THE GRIT FACTOR

THE GRIT FACTOR

COURAGE, RESILIENCE & LEADERSHIP IN THE MOST MALE-DOMINATED ORGANIZATION IN THE WORLD

SHANNON HUFFMAN POLSON

Harvard Business Review Press
Boston, Massachusetts

The web addresses referenced in this book were live and correct at the time of the book's publication but may be subject to change.

Library of Congress Cataloging-in-Publication Data

Names: Polson, Shannon Huffman, author.
Title: The grit factor : courage, resilience, and leadership in the most male-dominated organization in the world / Shannon Huffman Polson.
Description: Boston, MA : Harvard Business Review Press, 2020. | Includes index.
Identifiers: LCCN 2020010267 (print) | LCCN 2020010268 (ebook) | ISBN 9781633697263 (hardcover) | ISBN 9781633697270 (ebook)
Subjects: LCSH: Resilience (Personality trait) | Toughness (Personality trait) | Command of troops. | Leadership. | Sex discrimination against women. | United States—Armed Forces—Women.
Classification: LCC BF698.35.R47 P65 2020 (print) | LCC BF698.35.R47 (ebook) | DDC 158.1—dc23
LC record available at https://lccn.loc.gov/2020010267
LC ebook record available at https://lccn.loc.gov/2020010268

ISBN: 978-1-63369-726-3
eISBN: 978-1-63369-727-0

*Dedicated to the memory of Dougald and Tori MacMillan,
who gave me a home as a young lieutenant at Fort Bragg.*

For Peter, Sam, and Jude, who have my heart.

*For all the new, transitioning, and developing leaders
moving into their own new experiences, willing,
despite the resistance, to face into the wind.*

Contents

THE GRIT FACTOR

Introduction

Plotting a Course for Grit

A s I walk onto the flight line, the night sky is moonless, the darkness deep and menacing. I am walking with my backseater, the pilot who flies behind me in the tandem glass cockpit of our Apache, the world's most sophisticated attack helicopter. Each of our battalion's twenty-four Apaches crouches in its own fortified space, bounded by walls four feet tall and two feet thick, constructed of large stones held in place by chicken wire. These barriers will contain an explosion if a grenade is lobbed over the perimeter, limiting the damage. Two rows of fencing topped with barbed concertina wire define the perimeter of the flight line. This late at night, the Apaches are visible only as hulking shapes of latent energy. All are armed with Hellfire antitank missiles and 30 mm high-explosive rounds.

With each step, our eyes adjust to the darkness. We walk around the helicopter for one last check before climbing in to launch. We begin the run-up procedure, and I hear the rotor blades cut into the thick darkness and begin churning the air in a rhythmic *thump thump*.

I pull pitch, pulling up the lever of the collective that changes the angle of all four rotor blades simultaneously, and I feel a momentary lightness as our aircraft lifts into the air and we transition to forward flight. We move into the night, dark sky above shadowy ground, everything dark except for the green picture I see through the infrared monocle over my right eye. The infrared picture is clear and crisp, showing that the landscape is still holding the heat of Bosnia's Adriatic sun from just hours before. I call in to the tower to report departure, and fly us to the checkpoint just to the north of the airfield, a route we know now by heart.

"You have the controls," I say to my backseater.

"I have the controls," he confirms.

"You have the controls," I say again, all part of carefully scripted communications procedures.

Our communication is aural only. The positioning of our seats does not permit a questioning glance. Now I'm in charge of navigation. I open the large, folded map on my knee, and use my lips to turn on the tiny green light attached to my microphone. Under minimal illumination, I check and tune the radios for the next frequencies we will need, and confirm the waypoints I have programmed against the pencil line I've drawn along our route. I do all of this in less than a minute, actions carried out with little effort, a product of repeated drilling throughout training. As we fly north along our route, I check in with the ground units we're flying over in Multinational Division North, units from various NATO countries. The objective isn't far tonight. We begin to slow as we approach the area where we will perform an armed aerial reconnaissance of a Serbian heavy-weapon storage site.

Then, at that moment, in that night, in the midst of the radio calls coming from ground forces and from the air-traffic-controlling agency, the sound in my helmet changes.

"Radar . . . tracking . . ." the electronic voice says.

My backseater and I know immediately what the voice indicates. I feel my heart in my throat. We're being tracked by the most lethal antiaircraft system in the world.

"What do you want me to do LT?" my backseater asks. "Do you want me to break the hard deck?"

We had been briefed on our arrival into this country that the rules of engagement specified a minimum flight altitude, or hard deck, of three hundred feet, much higher than we are comfortable flying tactically because of the susceptibility to surface fire or antiaircraft weapons. Lower-altitude flying permits us to mask our movements and thus avoid enemy contact. The minimum altitude is meant to support the next operational phase of postwar Bosnia, the resettlement of the Muslim community previously forced out of homes and neighborhoods, by reducing the disruption to the civilian population.

"I'll call it in," I say, quickly tuning the VHF radio to reach the air-controlling agency.

I key the mike.

"This is Blue Max Five-Six. We're at position Alpha at three hundred feet, and we're getting a tracking signal from hostile radar," I report.

In the few seconds of waiting for the reply, the sound in my headset changes.

"Radar . . . acquisition . . ." comes the computerized voice.

Just then the voice at the controlling agency crackles back on the frequency.

"If you're nervous, return to base," the voice on the other end says. "But don't break the hard deck."

Nervous? Heck yes, we were nervous. I had a decision to make in that few seconds, a decision that had to take into account layers of information: Our threat briefs indicated a lowered threat level. No aircraft had been targeted in recent months. Provocation was more likely than engagement. Engagement would result in an international incident. In that instant, I had to make a choice not to allow myself to be paralyzed by fear, and instead to use the judgment developed by years of training to make a quick yet measured response.

What I did in the face of that challenge, the decision I made, I'll save for chapter 7. But I learned something that night, something I knew from other experiences outside the aircraft. When a leader encounters fear, and she will, she has to fly straight through it. As inevitable as fear may be, there's no room for it in that cockpit. The only way to avoid being sidetracked or taken down by fear is to do the opposite of what would seem natural. Instead of turning around, a leader turns toward fear and addresses it head-on.

The decision to turn toward fear instead of away from it takes grit, something I'd learned in childhood. Grit is a quality—and, as you'll discover, a skill—that more than any other has been critical to my successes. Now that I have been out of the military for more years than I served and have taken on new challenges, I've learned that most of the places that require grit aren't in the air. There are many situations that require you to adapt quickly, effectively, and often with little support—for your own sake, but also for the sake of those you are leading, whether by official position or by example. There are many situations that may seem, at first, impossible. How you address those situations, and your success in making the most of them, has a lot to do with this ingredient I grew up calling grit. Grit has many dimensions—character, courage, and conviction among them. Each of these is already within you, and each can be further developed. It takes grit to survive a hostile environment—in the air or in the boardroom—and it is also true that hostile environments develop grit.

Why I Wrote This Book

There is much I wish I'd known in those early years when I was developing the judgment that would serve me that night in Bosnia. As one of the first women to fly the Apache helicopter in the US Army, I found myself—in the mid-1990s, just out of college and flight school—in a field with no women to look to in senior positions, surrounded by people who did not, for the most part, want me there, and some who would make being there quite difficult. The internet wasn't yet common, so finding the stories of others who had persevered and triumphed wasn't easy. Few stories of other women in uniform had been told, and I was too overwhelmed to have the presence of mind to look for them. Had I looked, very few would have been available outside of quickly forgotten local-news headlines. Stories of women in uniform, their trials and triumphs, simply had not been the stories that were shared.

The requirements of the mission and the aircraft were demanding, and I thrilled to the challenge, but my greatest difficulties had nothing to do with flying, and it is there I would have given anything for thoughtful mentorship. Still today, stories and advice—or often, mentorship of any kind—are in short supply, especially for women in fields still mostly populated by men. This is true despite studies showing that women's ambitions match those of their male counterparts. I wrote this book for all women who lead or aspire to lead. Maybe you are one of these women, or you know one. I also hope that men running organizations will find important takeaways in these pages about successfully integrating women into leadership roles. I hope that by hearing stories of women overcoming seemingly insurmountable obstacles, in the most daring of professions, women who have succeeded and failed and always had twice as much to overcome—that in it all, you will be able to learn lessons about developing your own sense of grit, whether you are starting out, transitioning to new places in your careers, or facing challenges with little support.

I've been working on this book for over three years, starting about a decade after I took off the uniform. In those first ten years after I hung up my flight suit, I earned an MBA at the Tuck

School of Business at Dartmouth and worked in the field at Guidant in cardiac rhythm management, and then led teams at Microsoft. I left the corporate world to write my first book, *North of Hope*, a few years after a family tragedy (a story I will share more of later in the book), and then earned my MFA before beginning to write, and then speak, about the lessons and stories I was internalizing from years in both the corporate and military worlds.

Then one day, I received an email through an online officer-mentorship program. I'd been part of this program for only six months when I was asked to be available for the first women transitioning into submarines, but none of them contacted me. Then an inquiry came from a brand-new second lieutenant in the Army. She was just getting ready to start flight school, she said. Would I consider being her mentor?

I agreed immediately, and then had second thoughts. I'd been out for over ten years, and the challenges in my experience as one of the first women to fly Apaches in the Army were surely somewhat unique. I wanted to be able to offer her advice from a broader range of experience. I also knew that there must be other women who were seeking and could benefit from this kind of knowledge. How could I scale it to be available to others as well? These questions led to the idea that became the basis of this book. What if I were to interview other military women who were in the vanguards of their fields, women of varied branches and levels of experience, who could speak about grit—that factor I'd always thought of as critical to my success throughout the years—by telling their stories and offering concrete advice?

I started reaching out to other military women who, like me, had learned how to succeed in the most male-dominated organization in the world. The women interviewed for this book didn't join the military understanding the challenges ahead of them. The women who responded positively to my invitation to share their stories nearly all reported that they hadn't given much thought to what it meant to be the first woman in her role. As Captain Katie Higgins, the first woman to fly with the vaunted aerial demonstration team the Blue Angels, told me, "I didn't fathom the impact my joining the team would have. I was just there to do my job." General Ann Dunwoody, the first woman to achieve the rank of four-star general, had expected to spend her required two years in the Army and then get out and be a school PE instructor. But every one of these women, from World War II WASPs to early women combat pilots, submariners, rescue swimmers, and general officers all came to have an intimate understanding of grit, and the more holistic development that supports it. They learned how to weather change and uncertainty, make the most of difficult circumstances, and find the place inside of themselves that helps them persevere when things get tough.

Several of the younger leaders I interviewed spoke of the importance of a sisterhood, how they have been supported by it and how important it has been to their effectiveness and their longevity in the armed forces. Those of us in earlier generations did not have that advantage. Selfishly, *The Grit Factor* has been a way for me to connect to a sisterhood so completely lacking in my own experience. If you are currently the lone woman in your company, or even your field, I hope this book might be a sisterly companion for you as well. And if you are a man who manages one of these women, or if you love one of these women, I hope this book will help you understand both what she may be experiencing and how you can best support her.

The women I interviewed for this book generously offer stories and takeaways that apply in any circumstance of life or work. These women are examples, they are mentors, and by the end of this book, you might just feel as if they are friends. Unless otherwise noted, all remarks and recollections that I quote from these women in the ensuing chapters come from phone conversations I had with each over several years' time.

Why Grit, and Why Now?

Should we be focusing on grit? The psychologist Angela Duckworth's work on grit in her Character Lab at the University of Pennsylvania identified grit as a key component—if not *the* key component—of success, more than any other factor. This helped focus all of us on core character attributes and skills, going deep to find the sources of our strength. After the popularity of Duckworth's book *Grit* soared in the wake of her TED talk, there was a backlash. Why were we focused on grit when the focus should be on changing the system that demands this kind of exceptional tenacity of its minority members? In the wake of the #MeToo movement, this is an apt concern. It will take sustained effort and leadership from both men and women to change workplace culture. And sustained effort and leadership require—you guessed it—grit. In the midst of seemingly untenable challenges, grit will get us through the hardest times.

We must indeed work toward changing that reality, and yet the truth is that the world needs the best all of us have to offer right now, and that leaders today are facing challenges both in and out of uniform. I wrote *The Grit Factor* to help with both inspiration and tactical exercises to identify and develop the grit necessary to navigate these hardships.

While I expanded my cognitive understanding of grit thanks to Duckworth's provocative work, I found I needed more stories of real people who have faced circumstances similar to the challenges I was facing. I wanted to share stories, particularly of women who are in the minority among their peers and the people they are charged with leading.

After establishing a base familiarity with the current research, I began interviewing military women who had lived the challenges of leadership while also contending with hostilities within the system. I gathered their instructive and inspiring stories and listened to the lessons they learned. I wanted to be able to understand (and share) the particulars of grit, by talking to the grittiest women around. The military demands unparalleled focus, discipline, and sacrifice from those who choose to take the oath and wear the uniform. All of us whose stories went into this book experienced not only the rigorous challenges and responsibilities of military life but also the need to navigate the most insular and male-dominated organization in the country and our world. While wrestling with challenges in and out of combat zones along with their fellow soldiers, sailors, airmen, and Marines, the women featured in this book were forced to make their way through a world rarely welcoming and in many cases openly threatening. Ours was a double challenge, a layered crucible, and the stories and lessons that emerged come doubly forged. If anyone has something valuable to say about grit, it's a woman who has risen through the ranks of the most male-dominated organizations in the world.

Though all the women I interviewed for this book have a military background, the stories and insights they share will help anyone facing challenges with little support, whether that's navigating your way through the seismic change technology brings to so many fields, weathering an acquisition or reorganization, or getting through a difficult period with a project or work environment. This hypothesis is proved repeatedly with every audience I speak to around the country today, in industries ranging from finance to health care, logistics to produce, education to plastics.

You may be thinking that grit is a "you've either got it or you don't" trait, or the end result of surviving a lifetime of struggles— that the leaders featured in this book are simply extraordinary and unusual. But the good news is that grit is a skill. It can be developed. After years in uniform and years in the corporate world as well, I know for certain that grit is not reserved for military pilots and big-mountain climbers. Grit and resilience are innate to every single one of us. Like any skill, though, it may need to be nurtured and it must be maintained. Any of us can get out of practice. Fortunately both training and maintenance are possible.

To help you do that, I've organized the stories and the insights from my own experiences and research, and organized them into three categories: Commit, Learn, and Launch. Underneath these categories are eight aspects of grit. Each of these aspects gets its own chapter, which I've filled with relevant stories, research, and specific strategies and exercises meant to support and guide you in your own journey of grit.

How Grit Relates to Leadership

This is a book about leadership. It is a book about grit. Those who are first in their fields, or one of few in their fields, are leaders by virtue of circumstance, and the challenges ahead of them require grit. Their successes show others what is possible. Those who lead and are committed to making a difference either by choice or circumstance need grit, full stop.

I do have one warning for you: if you are looking for a one-size-fits-all leadership model, this book will disappoint. The leaders here are successful because they found a way to lead that is true to themselves, and they all are as unique as their own fingerprints. This is one of the biggest lessons, that becoming an authentic leader is a personal journey that will look different for everyone (something we will cover in depth in chapter 7). At the same time, these leaders do share some commonalities. Before taking on the most difficult work, these leaders did the work to own their own stories and to understand their environments. The other aspects of grit that they share we will cover in each successive chapter. These elements form the basis of *The Grit Factor.*

This is, at last, the book I would like to have had when I was starting out with no women to use as examples in my field, surrounded by men who in many cases, despite my performance, were reluctant at best to accept me as a colleague, much less as a leader.

I am deeply honored to share the stories of these remarkable women, and the lessons they learned, with you today, and am confident you will come away with specific advice that will help you excel at any stage of your career, as well as an invigorated and informed sense of purpose and passion.

Like anything both difficult and worthwhile, developing grit requires dedicated and consistent effort. It is my hope that the stories here animate the advice and lessons in a way that will make you excited to develop your courage and your resilience. Each chapter includes practical exercises, too, so that you can spend time with the lessons and apply them to your own circumstances. This combination of lesson, story, and tactical work is designed to help you develop grit in yourself. It's unlikely you are hearing enemy systems in your helmet in the middle of an Adriatic night, but you do and will have challenges that feel just as precarious. After reading and working through *The Grit Factor*, you will have what you need in yourself not only to make it through but to come out stronger.

Part One

COMMIT

— 1 —

Know Your Story

"If you don't like someone's story, you write your own."

—Chinua Achebe

I never imagined myself serving in military uniform. Our family's military history was limited to my father's four-year service as a JAG officer, drafted after law school for Vietnam and sent at the last minute to Alaska instead. Our family kept his uniformed photo on the wall and spoke of his service with pride.

Something in my dad connected more to serving than protesting, though the latter had been more the social norm during his college years in the 1960s. There was something of the contrarian in my father—something that led him to reject mediocrity and insist on doing things his own way even if it was hard. I always admired and respected these things about him.

As a lawyer in the military, he found himself, a small-town Kansas boy, surrounded by attorneys from prestigious schools. He told me that he realized if he prepared more and worked harder than anyone else, he could win the cases no matter what /

his opponent's pedigree. Once his service was over, he decided to stay in Alaska, breaking with his family's Midwestern roots, which would have dictated coming home and staying put. After working for a year in the Anchorage city attorney's office, he chose the harder route and struck out on his own, establishing a practice that has lasted past his death and retained his name. These are the parts of his story he shared with me, that stuck with me, that became a part of me.

These traits I inherited from my father—along with aspects of my own story—led me to the military. I was the eldest child, and in the late 1980s, my home state of Alaska still reeled from an economic recession, and my family reeled from divorce. When I filled out college applications—still on a typewriter—I remember my father asking me if I might be interested in one of the military academies, or in ROTC. I laughed it off, thinking the idea ridiculous, and my dad let it go. But when I arrived on the hot and humid gothic campus of Duke University in the fall of 1989, I lingered at the booths for ROTC at an activity fair. By then I'd taken out my college loans, discussed with my father the tight finances that were a part of college. I worked as a waitress at a campus restaurant and as a clerk at the campus housing office. I learned that the Army would allow me to major in the humanities and the scholarship it offered would help considerably with college costs. I decided to give Army ROTC a try.

What else went into that decision? In my high school years I'd found a way to escape my family drama by plunging myself into activities, both academics and sports. I was editor of the literary magazine, president of the debate club, and swim team captain. These diversions separated me from what was happening at home, but they also helped me realize that I loved the feeling of successfully meeting a challenge. I took on one activity after another, each time building on the accomplishments and insights of the one before. I thrived on the trials.

After my first year of college, ROTC gave me the opportunity to go to Airborne School, the three-week program at Fort Benning, Georgia, culminating in five static-line jumps out of an airplane. I was terrified—well before we even climbed into an airplane for the first time. I refused to jump off the 30-foot tower, requiring an instructor, with a boot to my backside, to ensure that I did. On my first jump from the massive C-130, I was in chalk 1, or the first group to jump. For the entire short flight, I stared at the chaplain who sat across from me. He was the first jumper out—the wind dummy. I silently mouthed the Lord's Prayer and a passage from Isaiah, sure I was catapulting to my death. Five jumps later, I earned my jump wings.

The next year at college, I started skydiving. Again, I was utterly terrified, cutting through the fear on each jump and learning to fly, moving my body against the air to make formations in the sky with my fellow jumpers—precision performance at terminal velocity. I'd dive through the clouds, and then float down under canopy looking out over the rolling North Carolina farmland. I loved the singularity of the experience, the repudiation of all I thought constrained my opportunities.

The summer after my sophomore year in college, I came home to the chance to join a climbing team heading for the summit of Denali in honor of the fiftieth anniversary of the Anchorage Rotary Club. It was youthful excitement and naivete that led me to join. (At age nineteen, I would become the youngest woman to summit Denali at the time, according to the rangers.) On the mountain, I thrilled to the adventure and the challenge. I realized I could get through the moments of terror, the excruciating difficulties, and that the reward of the journey made it all worthwhile. Somewhere in those years spent on the icy slopes of Denali and freefalling from thirteen thousand feet, I decided that I was not going to let fear circumscribe what was possible. With each opportunity to test myself, I became a little bit braver, and a little bit stronger.

All of this was a part of my story, even if I didn't understand it at the time. My social insecurities heightened at a traditional Southern university with unspoken rules and mores and a Greek system, all of which were utterly foreign to any of my lived experience, but as in high school, finding new challenges kept me focused on what was possible. My fellow ROTC cadets had worked to save for college, all during their childhoods and young adulthoods, the same as I had done. Wearing the uniform was alien to me, but connected to a story I knew and for which I had deep respect. Service was something that I understood. While the challenges seemed insurmountable at first, I knew that I'd overcome difficulties before. I'd conquered my fear. I'd picked myself up when I'd fallen. I could do it again.

I was commissioned a second lieutenant in the US Army the day before I received my diploma with a BA in English literature, on a humid spring day on the campus of Duke University. Later that year I reported to Fort Rucker, Alabama, the Army's flight school, and graduated with honors. From there I was assigned to my first duty station: Fort Bragg.

Crossing into the city limits of Fayetteville, North Carolina, on my way to Fort Bragg and Simmons Army Airfield in the spring of 1995, I sensed that I was entering a place of resistance. At twenty-three years of age, newly graduated from the Army's Initial Entry Rotary Wing course and the AH-64 Apache transition course, I had been assigned to the 229th Attack Aviation Regiment, part of the Army's storied XVIII Airborne Corps. I knew that out of 120 pilots in the regiment, I would be the only woman—the first such pilot in the history of the 229th. This was another challenge, I thought, like climbing Denali or skydiving, though I think even then I knew my understanding didn't extend nearly far enough.

What I entered driving through those gates was a culture and a story that fascinated me. I knew that the military story given to those who wear the uniform is one of selfless service and sacrifice, and that this story is what allows soldiers to do the incredible and seemingly impossible things required of them. I wanted to do the impossible.

What I didn't understand was that the military had another story, and that story said that only men could truly be soldiers. I assumed resistance was based on ignorance of women's capabilities, and I felt sure I could overcome that resistance. I did not understand that part of the military story was so deeply opposed to my existence within it that, by my audacity to put on a uniform and report, I was in some people's eyes violating centuries' of tradition foundational to the democratic republic that we served. My presence was an assault on tradition, and on the (mis)perceptions certain soldiers had that their exceptionalism was based in part on the exclusion of women from their work.

The first day I walked out on the tarmac toward the Apache helicopter, I thought it resembled a praying mantis more than a helicopter. The Apache is fifty-eight feet long, eighteen feet wide, and twelve feet high. Two 1,850-horsepower engines sit high on the fuselage, and three sight systems mounted on the nose allow for visibility during the day, the night, and adverse conditions. There are tandem seats for two pilots clearly visible in the all-glass cockpit. Three lethal weapon systems hang from the belly and the wings: the 30 mm cannon slewed to the pilots' helmets, the 2.75-inch folding-fin aerial rockets (FFAR), and the Hellfire antitank missiles. It is the most lethal and technologically advanced helicopter in the world. What was I doing there? What made me think I could fly this thing?

Right there, right then, on the tarmac, I had to make a decision. I had to believe I was better than any of the doubts I was feeling, the doubts I had heard others express about women—about me—climbing into the cockpit of the Apache. I had to take control of my own narrative and remind myself that I had chosen this path. I had earned my place. I was ready.

I walked out to that steel machine, put my left foot on the wheel, my right foot up onto the forward avionics bay, and turned the handle to open that all-glass cockpit. The door opened up and out like that of a Lamborghini. I reached in and grabbed the handholds of the steel frame of the cockpit, swung myself in, and lowered myself into the seat. I connected the five-point harness. I Velcroed my kneeboard onto my leg. And then I began the run-up procedure I would learn by heart—though we always used a checklist. Auxiliary power unit on. Engines on. Power levers advance. Let the rotors spin to full RPM. Release the brakes. Pull in collective, slightly forward on the cyclic, a little bit of right pedal. Taxi out onto the tarmac, and turn in the direction of takeoff.

Writing about this time, it's almost impossible to use the pronoun *I*. That is part of the military story, too—the individual is subsumed in the organization. Whether or not I was accepted as a part of the organization, I was required to think of myself as part of it. It would take me some time to understand this institutional story, and how my own story might coexist with it. Yet, without knowing my own story, I would never have been able to weave myself into the narrative that existed inside the boundaries of that legendary Army base.

Before a soldier is able to truly understand herself as part of a larger narrative, she has to understand her own narrative, as does anyone who wants to go the distance in any field—corporate, nonprofit, or personal. To be effective and to truly lead, she has to continue to understand her own story, both the degree to which it exists as a thing apart, and how it exists within the larger whole.

Why Story Matters

The Army leadership model is to "Be, Know, Do." The "Be" refers to understanding and believing in yourself, your mission, and the Army, and integrating precepts of leadership into your character. On one extreme, "being" involves becoming something other than what you are, and there is no question that starting from basic training the job is to remake an individual into a soldier. But operating apart from who you are is neither tenable in the long term nor desirable. In the process of becoming, to believe in yourself, you first have to understand yourself. Even in the military, where the group is esteemed above all else, understanding yourself has to precede integration into the larger whole. The same holds true in the corporate world—before you are ready to lead others to achieve the aims of the group, you need to do the work to understand, craft, and own your own story.

Story shapes and holds traditions, ancient and new, compelling both action and emotion. Young children who beg their parents for one more bedtime story inherently know the power of narrative to define their understanding, to form their soul, though they would not be able to say it in quite that way. The same is true for anyone who binge-watches serial dramas on TV, can't put down a novel, or listens to one of the hundreds of thousands of podcasts that have debuted since the form came into being in 2004.

So stories are not simply this fabric of childhood. Perhaps a better understanding of story is that the stuff of childhood has power beyond what we could ever have imagined. Story is the core of identity: defining nations and kings, queens, and soldiers, mothers and fathers, poets and engineers. Story is also the stuff of action: acts of war and works of genius, death-defying expeditions and brutal campaigns. It is an essential force for all human beings, past, present, and future.

Harvard folklorist Maria Tatar studies the fairy tales all children have heard, and she finds that many recur across centuries, cultures, and continents in one form or another, all a part of what she calls "the great cauldron of story." In an interview with Krista Tippett, host of the NPR program *On Being*, Dr. Tatar says, "these stories change in wonderfully productive ways. And they do get us talking about our values . . . they help us develop a kind of moral compass."[1] We may not consciously understand why stories matter. We only know we crave them—even those we have heard told myriad ways before—as shown by the popularity of the series *Grimm*, *Once Upon a Time*, and *Game of Thrones*.

Marketers apply the power of story quietly and effectively, by creating stories with images. Sometimes they do so even more overtly, as in the Title Nine catalog, where pictures are accompanied by each model's name and one or two interesting facts about her. The outdoor brand Patagonia incorporates relevant articles in its product catalogs, while making sustainability a powerful part of its brand story. The eponymous J. Peterman catalog created fictional vignettes around illustrated product images.

Recent media ventures—the now near ubiquitous TED talks, National Public Radio's *StoryCorps* and *The Moth Radio Hour*, and the invitation-only Future of StoryTelling conference—are just a few indications of our hunger for story and our renewed appreciation for its underpinning of our lives and consciousness. Politicians, like marketers, have always known about the power of story in all of its complexity. Political consultant and lecturer Marshall Ganz of Harvard is known for his storytelling formula employed in the Obama presidential campaign.[2]

Simply put, stories help us survive. I wrote my first book, *North of Hope*, a memoir that traces my journey on an Arctic river in Alaska following the route my father and stepmother had traveled the year before when they were killed by a grizzly bear in their tent, because I needed a lifeline. The shock was almost too much for me, and I was not alone. Over the days and weeks that followed, I'd meet others who knew my dad and stepmother and who lived with that special kind of horror that comes from such a violent and gruesome event. The need to write *North of Hope* was clear—I had to find a way to take the circumstances that I had been given, and work honestly with the unwanted and painful reality until something beautiful could come of it. I had to, quite literally, write my own story. I had to find a way toward hope in the midst of the darkness, and pray that it might be helpful to others as well. Crafting the story was critical to my survival at that juncture. But it is just as important to make sense of your story when you are facing more quotidian challenges. In fact, you are hardwired to do so.

The Science of Story

Our innate knowledge as well as recent scientific advances show how we humans cocreate our lives through the development of both individual and collective narratives. Over the last few decades, neuroscience has shed light on why story matters to us as much as it does.

Story forms the foundation for the field of narrative psychology, which is the field behind narrative identity, a critical piece of understanding one's life in the context of story. That story is not simply a timeline of a life, not the accrual of incidents, but instead is the way you construct an identity using the raw material of your life events. It is the challenge, the opportunity, and perhaps even the mandate to take the pieces of a life and put them together honestly and in a positive and productive way that not only explains the past, but also helps to create the future.

Stories help us make sense not only of ourselves, but also of the people with whom we share the world. Recent research using brain imaging shows a tight correlation between the activity of our brains in listening to and processing story, on the one hand, and interacting with other people and navigating relationships on the other.[3] Scientists call the ability of the brain to map others' intentions "theory of mind," and stories teach us how to do it.

The importance of both creating and integrating narratives is foundational to leadership. Northwestern University psychologist Dan McAdams, an expert on narrative identity, found that "internalizing the stories you create about yourself is a key source of personal strength and meaning." He also found that we can reframe our stories in order to "adopt a positive identity," one that will help you persist even when you aren't getting the positive results your story has led you to seek.[4]

Forming a cohesive and ongoing personal narrative appears to be a fundamental role of our brains, particularly the left hemisphere, which serves as what cognitive neuroscientist Michael Gazzaniga, a professor of psychology at the University of California, Santa Barbara, and a pioneer in the study of hemispheric (left and right brain) thinking, describes as "the Interpreter"—an organizer of our memories into plausible stories.[5] Once formed, these stories help us navigate the world; to know where we're coming from and where we're headed.

Our minds form stories out of the disparate elements of our experience, whether we decide to play an active part in the construction of those stories or not. There is a strong overlap among the functions of remembering, imagining, and predicting the future going on inside our minds nearly all the time.[6] This explains why two people can remember a shared experience so differently.

By taking the time to construct a story that makes sense of your history, you also provide yourself a tool for creating a future that matches the trajectory of that narrative. If you don't proactively take control of your own narrative, you will get buffeted by the stories your organization, family, or society will tell. Women across roles and industries in the corporate world share the stories they've been told: *You shouldn't be so ambitious. You shouldn't apply for that promotion. You have no business in a man's world. You're not vulnerable enough. You're too pushy. You're too emotional.* Those stories come from work environments as well as from families of origin or peer groups. Only by writing the story of your own grit will you be able to shape your own success—as opposed to merely hoping it will happen.

Creating your own narrative requires self-awareness, and lays the groundwork for defining your purpose, a companion piece to story and grit that we'll explore in chapter 2.

Your Story Can Propel
You through Resistance

In every one of her assignments through her three decades of service, Lieutenant General Claudia Kennedy was the first woman to hold her position. She began her career in the Women's Army Corps, commissioned in 1969 with a degree in philosophy. From the outset, the possibilities for her success seemed limited.

"When I joined the military," she recalls, "it was rare for women to rise to lieutenant colonel. Beyond that was almost unimaginable."[7]

Still, Kennedy was the daughter of a soldier, and as the Vietnam War was at its height, she felt strongly that women should also make sacrifices to support the country. Yet she admits that she didn't at first realize that the military only offered roles for women that diminished and demeaned their service and their presence. In one instance, Kennedy remembers that when she was selected to be a general's aide, she understood that she had been chosen from an "LSD" folder. When inquiring about the LSD folder, she was told it stood for "Little Sexy Doll."

Recognizing the challenges she faced with greater clarity after her first few years of service, Kennedy sat down with the officer assigned to be her career counselor and asked him about possibilities for her next several assignments.

"Your career path is very circumscribed, captain," the officer told her. "You women will never get anywhere in the Army until the male chauvinist pigs like me are out."

Kennedy said the only thing she could have at that point: "Yes, sir."

Inside, though, she rejected the story she'd been told and wrote her own story on the spot.

"I looked the officer in the eye and thanked him for his time. *You can't run me out of the Army*, I thought. *I'll be here long after you are gone.*"[8]

It was Kennedy's story that prevailed: she continued a long, exemplary career and became the first woman to rise to the rank of lieutenant general (three stars) in the Army.

Kennedy faced—indeed was serving inside of—an institutional story that excluded her from the possibility of meaningful contribution. While an existing social or cultural narrative might carry a more traditional leader along with it like the tide, these narratives are historically exclusive of large parts of the population. Like the tide, these existing stories are powerful beyond measure, and nearly impossible to resist, unless you consciously create a different story.

The leaders I interviewed for this book all entered fields dominated by men. Because the existing cultural narratives did not include women, these leaders faced the double challenge of not only creating their own stories but also developing narratives running directly counter to institutional narratives that often narrowly limited these leaders' opportunities, abilities, and potential. Even outside the military, women and members of other minorities all too often experience resistance to their very presence and to their audacious willingness to push limits set by a majority. This resistance can be disrespectful and denigrating. Your commitment to claiming your own story must be stronger than the pushback you experience from those around you. That commitment requires often unacknowledged but nevertheless substantial work to fight an existing narrative while also doing your job. Having a story about yourself that reminds you of who you are, what your strengths are, and what you're capable of makes this work less arduous and more successful. It's no wonder that each leader I interviewed for this book talks of her life as a kind of story, or at least identifies the key elements of story as critical to her path.

Understanding the story of your life and how you're choosing to live it is part of connecting to grit. This narrative will be a place you can return to as needed to find your way through difficulty. The best part—as well as the hardest—is that you get to write it yourself.

How to Write—or Reframe—Your Own Story

Stories may occur spontaneously to you in a moment of insight or challenge, as Kennedy's did. More commonly, though, understanding your story will take thoughtful reflection. Discovering your life's narrative requires going back to the beginning. Once you can articulate your values and your strengths and weaknesses, you can proactively capitalize on those areas where you are strongest and reinforce areas of weakness. When you craft your story, identifying your values and purpose, this story becomes a place to which you can repeatedly return to find strength in the midst of hardship.

A writer considers the way that a story moves, and thinks of it as a shape, often called a narrative arc. Within that arc might be any number of turns, but in every case there will be a conflict of some kind—a challenge, a problem, a crisis—encountered by a character. The conflict functions as an inflection point. Both the movement of the story and the development of the character involved must change. Each character development has an arc, too—a character does not move through a story, or navigate a conflict, and come out the same person. The key to narrative identity is to claim your own arc, the narrative arc of your life story. The shape of your arc not only tells the story of your past—it also helps to point you toward your future.

(I'll walk you through a personal-narrative exercise at the end of this chapter.)

It is likely, whether you realize it or not, that you already have a story about yourself—one that may not be particularly supportive. The good news is that you can recreate the story so that the narrative works *for* you instead of against you.

"You're both the narrator and the main character of your story," Jonathan Adler, an assistant professor of psychology at Olin College, told *The Atlantic*. "That can sometimes be a revelation—'Oh, I'm not just living out this story, I am actually in charge of this story.'"[9]

The understanding that it is possible to reframe your own story was key to the success of pioneering Naval aviator Karen Fine Brasch. Brasch was in college, and thought of herself as a Texas "girly girl," perhaps the least likely to join the military. Aviation was in her blood, though. One of four girls born to an Air Force–fighter pilot father, Brasch had wanted to fly since she was nine years old. Her father humored her, taking her to the local municipal airport in Plano, Texas, to watch planes take off and land.

Still, she didn't set a path for the military. She worked full-time in college to pay her bills, but on one particularly tough day, she stood in the elevator heading to class and noticed a poster that read, "Learn to fly with Bubba."

"I took the poster off the wall, skipped class, drove over to the little airfield, set the paper on the guy's desk, and said, 'I want to learn to fly,'" she tells me when we talk by phone.

"He took one look at me and laughed," she says. "I was a twenty-one-year-old, big-haired sorority girl." Finally, the instructor composed himself, and offered to take Brasch up flying on the spot.

"I was wearing a jeans miniskirt and holding a can of Diet Coke," she remembers. "We preflighted and got in the aircraft. I remember handing him my Diet Coke because I had nowhere to put it. He just laughed. So I dumped it out and put the can on my lap. He gave me the controls and told me to take off. I did."

She was hooked.

After eight lessons Brasch started her application to the Navy's Aviation Officer Candidate School (AOCS) at Naval Air Station Pensacola, on Florida's panhandle. That's where things started getting tough.

When Brasch arrived in Pensacola, the first thing she noticed was the sign hanging over the entrance: "Adversity tempers steel."

"That phrase became the voice in my head over my flying career, as I sought one challenge after another," says Brasch. And she would need its guidance right away. "As we lined up to enter training, a big burly instructor came up behind me and grabbed the car keys hanging from my shaking hand. 'Trying to get away already?' he boomed. 'You won't be needing these any-more.' Strangely enough, I wasn't nervous anymore. It felt like an acknowledgment that my new adventure was beginning.

"I could not have been more of a fish out of water," Brasch continues. "I had hair down to the middle of my back, and they cut it all off. I did not fit in. I remember some silly swim competition where I was picked last. I was weak academically. I was weak physically. But I never quit."

The Marine drill sergeants running AOCS had no patience for weakness.

"I had a lot of extra time with the drill instructors," Brasch remembers. "But I did not want to be treated any differently just because I was a woman."

There were many more challenges to come. One was the fifteen-foot high dive where AOCS candidates had to jump in with full flight gear and swim twenty meters underwater without coming up for air.

"I wouldn't jump off of it," Brasch says. "I was inexplicably ter-rified. Another woman was assigned to walk me down to the pool every day and sit there while I waited to go jump and swim. I wasn't allowed to speak. She just marched me there, and I would stand on the high dive and stare down at the pool—paralyzed with fear and unable to jump. One day I decided she shouldn't have to babysit me anymore. It was one more thing I needed to do. I thought to myself, 'There's always going to be one more thing, so what the heck?' I jumped. It was her quiet support that helped me jump."

Whatever the Navy threw at her, however unprepared she was at times, "I was one hundred percent all in," Brasch says. "The only thing I wanted to do was fly. I was going to do whatever hard work was required to get there."

Another requirement of all candidates was getting over an eight-foot wall on an obstacle course without assistance. Brasch couldn't do it.

Faced with expulsion if she didn't scale the obstacle, a small group of women including Brasch realized that there was a wall in the barracks showers exactly the same height as the obstacle they were required to climb.

"After all the other women went to bed, we would run at this concrete wall in the shower," she says. "There wasn't room to get much of a running start, but we worked it anyway. We practiced so much we were bruised all the way down our sides, but it worked. I remember the day I went out and got myself over the obstacle. The drill instructor stood back and just said 'Oh. My. God.'"

Despite the many more challenges to come, Brasch had done the work to transform her understanding of herself from a "girly girl" co-ed to a Naval aviator. She committed herself completely to what was required. She changed her story. Despite falling along the way, she committed herself to success and wrote a new story. Brasch went on to retire from the Navy after twenty years, at the rank of commander.

When someone asks Brasch how she managed to become a pilot, her answer is simple, but holds all of the story she has lived. "It never occurred to me that I couldn't," she says. "I just really wanted it. I believed I could do it, when no one else did.

"Grit isn't something you learn," Brasch continues. "It's something you do. It starts out by something feeling impossible or overwhelming, requires all of your focus and fortitude while you're going through it, and it feels like you're going to fail right up to the very point you succeed. And you do it alone."

What she doesn't see as a solo job is sharing stories that help others to succeed. Outside of her work as a technical program manager, a mother of three, and an aspiring cellist, Brasch works today to help tell the story of the WASPs—the just over one thousand civilian women pilots known as the Women Airforce Service Pilots—who tested and ferried aircraft and trained pilots for the Army during World War II.

"What started as a small droplet of water with a few courageous women has turned into ripples that are turning into waves that will eventually reach the shore. Small numbers of women have made a significant impact for future generations," she tells me.

"We need to tell the story of holy hell . . . look what we did. It was hard, but look at the impact—look what we can still do. You can't stop us now." The story of courage and barrier-breaking that these trailblazing women achieved includes a lot of sacrifice, heartache, blood, sweat, and tears. It also includes a lot of women who signed up for military service, knowing that they were a minority and took on that challenge with gusto.

"It is time to tell the story," Brasch continues. "The good. The bad. And the ugly. Not just about victims and heroes. But the story of impact. What we did right. What we did wrong. Some of us were heroes. Some of us were villains. Some of us succeeded. Some of us failed. Some of us just did our job and moved on. But the full story. *The story of how a few created the many.*"

EXERCISE

Craft Your Story

1. Begin by writing out a timeline of your life from birth to present. Write down all meaningful events, both positive and negative, with positive events above the line, and negative

events below it. There is no external rule about what makes an event meaningful, other than that it had an impact on you.

Next to the positive events, write down what you did to participate in what made those events successful. Next to the negative events, write down what you learned as a result.

(handwritten note in margin: WHAT MIGHT BE TRUE?)

2. Now give each of those events a word indicating a value to you. Perhaps your parents divorced, and the value you still hold dear is *family*. Perhaps you were promoted after an intense period of challenging work, and the value that is meaningful for you is *perseverance*.

3. What themes emerge? What strengths can you discern? What do the values you've listed say about you? What are you particularly proud of?

4. How do these themes tell the story of your life? How might you tell the story of your life with a narrative arc that has been guided by those values?

5. Shift your focus from the past to the present and ask how the strengths you identified could help you in a current pursuit.

(handwritten note in margin: how haven't thought this!)

6. Now predict your future. Once you can articulate your own narrative identity, you can proactively plan to capitalize on those areas where you are strongest and reinforce areas of weakness. Can you identify strengths that are consistent or that have continued to develop throughout your life? Maybe it's working with or encouraging others, getting the job done, doing the behind-the-scenes work. Keep these in mind and ensure you find roles playing to those strengths. Are there weaknesses you might identify? How can you surround yourself with people who have the skills to compensate for those weaknesses? Might you spend time developing some of those weaknesses into strengths? How will the story of your life before prepare you well for your biggest goals?

Defining your personal narrative is not an exercise in journalism, not a cool reporting of facts. While it's important to be as honest with yourself as you can as you seek to discern the narrative arc in your own stories, you also have to decide how to weight different aspects of your story for the sake of the trajectory you want that story to set you on. For example, if you were a fearful child and now are embarking on a new role that scares you, you don't have to make the fact that you were once scared a major plot point, unless you are telling the story of your own growth and pivot. Consider also integrating the memories of the time you felt afraid but persisted anyway. Then your story becomes not about the fear, but about your bravery.

Your narrative is the story of how you have reacted to what has happened to you. It is how you have picked yourself up after failure, and how you have moved through and past challenges. It is the story of who, after all of these things, you have become. It is the story, too, of what you might do. Your story, at the end, is the one you write.

— 2 —

Drill Down to Your Core Purpose

"Everything can be taken from a man but one thing:
the last of the human freedoms—to choose one's attitude in
any given set of circumstances, to choose one's own way."

—Viktor E. Frankl

The small town of Dahlonega, Georgia, with its historic Southern buildings and brick-lined sidewalks, sits atop metamorphic rock formed from sediment put under extreme pressure hundreds of millions of years ago. The town holds enough gold that the United States established a small branch mint that operated there in the mid-1800s. The Chattahoochee-Oconee National Forests cover the rocky mountains in which Dahlonega is nestled. This land is the one-time home of the Creek and Cherokee tribes, whose descendants are scattered throughout the region. Today, the town hosts several small colleges. A few local wineries draw tourists.

Just outside of Dahlonega, fewer than half of the Army's toughest soldiers who began Ranger School three hours to the south, at Fort Benning, undergo the second phase of Ranger School, known as the mountain phase. These candidates are not thinking of the Southern charm mere miles away. They know only fatigue, hunger, and extreme exertion.

The wooded slopes of the mountains hold in the darkness and the heavy summer heat, and both press in on the Ranger candidates in the midst of rigorous training with little food or sleep. Ranger School is the crucible for leaders in the Army's combat arms. The Army website says that Ranger School "is one of the toughest training courses for which a Soldier can volunteer." The mountain phase of Ranger School is sixty-one days of just under twenty hours of training a day, with candidates consuming only one to two meals a day and carrying between sixty-five and ninety pounds.

In 2015, US Army infantry officer Shaye Haver was one of the first two women to attempt—and finish—the challenge. It was an experience that she very nearly didn't complete. It wasn't only the difficulties of hunger, fatigue, and extreme effort in a mountainous environment Haver was battling. Ranger School had only been opened to women earlier that same year, a move that unleashed a clamor of criticism.

When we talk by phone the first time, Haver remembers one particular night that tested her faith in herself.

"The RI [Ranger instructor] put us on a path and told us we were going to walk carrying a heavy pack until the sun rose. We didn't know where we were going, or how long.

"I don't know what it was about that night," she continues. "Maybe it was just fatigue. Those thoughts of being afraid, not staying in touch with why I was there, asking myself if I had what it took to finish . . . all those came up. It was really hot, and my ears started to get muffled. There was a pounding in my ears.

"I was thinking, I'm probably the slowest one out here, and suddenly I thought: I can't hear! I'm going deaf! I panicked. I started looking around, but I couldn't see anything. It was so dark. I couldn't figure out if I was lost or if I was blind, and still I had this pounding in my ears. I was freaking out. I thought: I'm just going to sit down. I felt like I was literally being crushed. I started thinking about the word *truth*. I can't be blind. I kept looking around, but I couldn't see anything in the darkness.

"I was talking to myself, murmuring. If anyone could have seen me, they would have thought I was crazy," she laughs. "That's when I had a come-to-Jesus moment. I asked myself: why am I here?"

From the start, the odds had been against Haver. Historically, less than 50 percent of all Ranger candidates pass the grueling course, and her class faced even worse odds. Along with 75 percent of her class, she had already been "recycled," or forced to repeat a training phase.[1]

Yet Haver had prepared tirelessly. She had, for years, been a competitive triathlete and weight-lifter, and had spent recent months preparing specifically for Ranger School with targeted physical work and mental training in the Army's Resilience Training program. She had trained for exactly these types of moments of desperation, fatigue, and doubt. She had formed, and was living, her own narrative.

In that panic-fueled moment, her deeper wisdom kicked in, reminding her why she was there in the first place.

"I reminded myself, I'm here for the ground soldiers," she says. "I'm a pilot, and I have to know how to support them. And I'm here for my mom—she's always had faith in me, and I haven't ever failed her. Then I started naming every one of my soldiers and the girls I started Ranger School with. I thought of all those people whose respect meant more to me than the feelings of doubt I was having. I got up, still not seeing anything, and started running."

Then she looked up.

"I was heading up a hill," she says, "and there was the beginning of day lighting the top of the hill, and an RI standing there a hundred meters above. I looked behind me, and I wasn't lost. Because I'd been running, I was in the lead.

"All these things I believed weren't true. I wasn't blind, I wasn't deaf. It was a new day. I got to start all over again.

"I'm grateful for that moment," she says. "It showed me how I react to pain, to fear, to being overwhelmed. Outside of combat, I don't think I ever would have experienced that."

Haver went on to graduate from Ranger School in August 2015, one of the first women to earn the coveted Ranger tab (along with her friend Captain Kristen Griest).

What got Haver through that long, dark night is the same thing that can get you through challenges too: she remembered why she was on that dark mountainside. She remembered the people who believed in her, and the people she worked with. She remembered the other women with whom she was undertaking such rigorous training. In other words, she remembered her purpose.

Purpose Is Bedrock to Grit

Clarity of purpose gives you the passion and commitment you need to navigate those inevitable moments of hardship, resistance, or change and to focus your efforts toward influence and impact. Purpose is the core of your story. It is bedrock to grit.

Identifying your purpose and your story (the story you uncovered in the previous chapter) becomes your foundation that ensures you stay committed to any undertaking that is in alignment with who you are and what you are on this earth to do. The combination is the point of departure for great leadership. Before getting to how you find it, let's look at what purpose is.

The etymology of the word *purpose* reaches back into the 1200s, from the Old French *porpos* and Anglo-French *purpos*, both origins referring to aim and intention. It is why you care, why you do what you do, and why you persevere when the going gets tough. It is the base of your being. Yet, as Haver's story reflects, purpose is always bigger than a single person. In her seminal work, *Grit*, Angela Duckworth writes, "Most gritty people see their ultimate aims as deeply connected to the world beyond themselves."[2] In other words, gritty people work for something greater—they have purpose.

To better define what purpose is and why it matters, I reached out to Aaron Hurst, CEO of Imperative and author of *The Purpose Economy*. I was fascinated by his writing about purpose as a primary driver in the twenty-first century, as well as by his related background as the founder of Taproot, which connects seasoned professionals to nonprofits for free consulting—a service I had tried while working to bring a new library to our small rural community. Aaron cheerfully welcomed me to his office in a converted loft in Seattle's Pioneer Square. From our conversation as well as his writing, it is clear that Hurst sees purpose as multidimensional.

People are seeking "more meaning in their lives," Hurst says. "This sense of meaning, or purpose, is driven by three specific and connected needs. Meaning comes from making an impact through our work, facing challenges and growing as individuals, and having strong relationships with those around us. The latter is the greatest source of meaning in our lives."[3]

Hurst is quick to point out that purpose comes from "within you, it's not something from outside of you. So a lot of people for example think purpose is about working in a nonprofit, or working in education, or being a social worker, or a nun." But these external things aren't purpose. They are what Hurst refers to as "causes," or areas that you care about. It's fine to have a cause, but your purpose is what makes you care about that cause in the first place. Purpose is your source of strength.

Purpose is not something that is given to you—at least not overtly. Each of us has to do the work to discern and then commit to our own purpose. Not everyone is purpose-driven, but gritty people are. Hurst offers this differentiation between people who are purpose-oriented and those who are not: "Purpose-oriented people are people that have the courage and the psychological disposition to be willing to really embrace purpose." This disposition—having courage and the willingness to do the right thing—are also key components of grit.

Having a clear sense of purpose doesn't just benefit you, it sends positive ripples through the work you do, too. Hurst finds a clear connection of purpose to performance in the data from a study he copublishes annually with NYU, called the Workforce Purpose Index. The data shows that on every measure, purpose-driven employees are the most valuable members of a workforce, with significantly longer tenure, higher work satisfaction, higher likelihood of assuming leadership positions, and higher likelihood of supporting their employees. Not surprisingly, purpose-driven employees perform much better on their performance reviews as well.

When retired Navy commander Darlene Iskra studied women general officers, she also identified the importance of purpose, publishing her findings under the title *Breaking through the Brass Ceiling*.[4]

When I correspond with Iskra, she automatically validates the same aspects of purpose Hurst has examined as key to the success of the general officers she interviewed.

These leaders "stayed in the service as long as they felt they were making a contribution, making a difference," she says. "If it had been 'too hard' or if they had not had family support or a feeling of camaraderie with their work mates, they would not have stayed the course. Resilience was a very important part of their success. Many used phrases like 'bloom where you are planted,' or 'when life gives you lemons, make lemonade.' Generals are a different breed not only because of self-selection and the ability to see beyond their current situation, but also due to the support they had from coworkers and superiors."

As Ranger-trained Shaye Haver's story shows, sometimes the awareness of purpose arises as a natural response to hardship. Ideally, you'll already have a clear understanding of your purpose before you encounter your next big test. Fortunately, there is a simple—not easy, necessarily, but simple—exercise that can help you get closer to identifying your own purpose. While grit is innate to every one of us, it is also developed by doing the work and developing the skills necessary to its exercise when the time comes. Part of that work is identifying your purpose.

Digging into Core Purpose: Connecting the Head and the Heart

For the leaders I interviewed for this book, all of whom surmounted the inherent difficulties posed by the nature of their military service and by being one of the first women in an environment where they were often unwelcome, having a strong sense of purpose was a critical element of success. These leaders knew—or learned quickly—that in order to succeed, they had to begin asking that single-word question: why? Beginning by answering this question allowed them to transcend challenging circumstances and achieve perseverance, momentum, and optimal performance.

Friedrich Nietzsche once said that "he who has a why can endure any how." Your purpose is your "why." In my experience, however, asking why often doesn't go far enough. Sometimes doing so only scratches the surface, revealing what Aaron Hurst calls the cause as opposed to the purpose. To dig deeper, deep enough to discover your core purpose, to connect your intellectual sense of purpose with your core purpose, ask yourself why you do what you do not once but five times. Yes, five.

I first learned of the Five Whys as a technique developed by Taiichi Ohno, the founder of the Toyota Production System. Ohno used the Five Whys as a technique to drill down into deficiencies, to permit a deeper look into problems. This practice of asking the Five Whys became standard at Toyota and later became part of the Six Sigma training program. By the repetition of inquiry into a given defect, Toyota found itself better able to determine the root causes of failures and avoid creating further problems brought on by quick, surface-level analyses.

How does a manufacturing tactic relate to purpose? By its insistence on getting to root cause, or in this exercise, to core purpose.

Your purpose addresses the task at hand. It considers what you are doing now, and why you're doing it. Your *core* purpose goes deeper. Your core purpose is what drives you today and every day. It is foundational to who you are, what makes you unique, what forms the core of your being. Your story informs your core purpose, and your core purpose informs the future of your story. In the face of so many competing distractions, discerning core purpose takes quiet and focused attention.

In writing workshops I lead, I use an exercise to introduce the concept of the long, hard look—a necessary step to get to the core truths or meaning the writers are seeking to convey, even if they think they already know. I ask participants to turn toward someone they don't know, and to look directly into their eyes without looking away for a full minute (sometimes two). By the end of the exercise, some participants are squirming, some trying not to laugh, others concentrating hard on pushing through the discomfort. The process is awkward at best, but it can make us realize that the hard look may require us to get uncomfortable. Most of us aren't willing to face the places in ourselves that might be challenging, pieces of ourselves that we have worked to ignore for any number of reasons. But in writing, as in leadership (and in all of life), we often have to push ourselves to delve deeper than daily life allows in order to find the meaning hidden beneath the surface.

The Five Whys is similar, forcing the long, hard look, beyond and beneath "cause" and even "purpose" in a specific situation, to discover core purpose. By continuing your investigation into purpose until you've drilled down five layers, you'll have moved past the superficial, finding the bedrock of what matters most to you. I will walk you through the Five Whys exercise at the end of this chapter so that you can experience it for yourself. But first I'll share how it helped me persevere during a challenging time that may be more relatable than anything having to do with flying an Apache: feeling myself growing stagnant in an unfulfilling job.

Finding Core Purpose during Everyday Struggles

Shaye Haver found insight into her core purpose during a high-stakes situation. For me, it was a more quotidian challenge that helped remind me of my purpose—perhaps a situation to which many people first starting out in their careers can relate. My job was neither interesting nor challenging. I wanted more opportunity.

When I reported for duty to Fort Bragg, North Carolina, I was twenty-three, newly graduated from Officer Basic Course, the Initial Entry Rotary Wing course, and the Apache attack-helicopter transition course. I was ready to fly and excited to lead my first platoon.

Arriving at Fort Bragg, I was the first woman assigned to the regiment, the only woman out of 120 combat pilots. I was assigned not to the platoon I had hoped for, but instead to serve as the assistant to the assistant S-3 operations officer, of 3rd Battalion,

229th Attack Aviation Regiment. I worked for a captain who assigned me to type up presentations and appendixes to operations orders. It was not without value, but it was a long way from where I thought I would have been. The work soon became deadening, and my frustration heightened when I learned secondhand what a lieutenant in our sister battalion was saying—that I hadn't been assigned a platoon because I wasn't up for it. Never mind that I knew the other lieutenant to be solidly mediocre in every sense. I talked to the captain I was working for, asking him when a platoon might be possible. He looked up from his desk impatiently.

"Lieutenant," he said, "the Army doesn't owe you anything."

I realized with a pang of despair that just because I had been trained didn't mean I would get the chance I had hoped for to be an aviation leader.

Even so, I remembered the adage passed down by my dad, who had learned it from his parents, who came from farm country in Kansas: if you're scrubbing toilets for twenty-five cents, you'd better earn every penny of that doing the best job you can. I knew that regardless of my disappointment, I had to excel at what I was doing and fight against my frustration. To do that, I had to find a way to connect to my core purpose—and I did it by asking the Five Whys.

When I first asked myself why I was where I was, why I was doing what I was doing, I started with:

"I'm here to fly and fight in the Apache helicopter and be an Army aviation leader."

That might motivate me temporarily, but it was easy to get stuck in the frustration of what I was not doing: flying and fighting in the Apache helicopter. Becoming an aviation leader may have been my purpose (though from Aaron Hurst's perspective, that job-related answer reflected more of a cause than a purpose), but I was not yet presented with the opportunity to do so, and I had little control over the decisions made. Without being able to change my circumstance, the only option I had available to keep me motivated in my work was connecting to my core purpose. I kept asking the question.

Why did I want to fly and fight in the Apache helicopter and be an aviation leader?

- Because I'm trained to do so.

    - Why?

- Because I earned and requested the training.

    - Why?

- Because I wanted to serve my country.

That was a pretty good place to land, but given that I had signed up to join the Army, it was also a little bit too obvious. I forced myself to ask one more time:

    - Why?

- Because I wanted to serve.

Boom! That was it.

I'd grown up in a patriotic family of Midwestern origin. But more important, I had grown up in a family for which faith and the idea of service were important. As a child, I visited retirement homes with my mother, made sandwiches with our youth group for those who didn't have enough to eat, and drove with my father to deliver food to families who needed it on a Christmas Eve.

I once asked my father, who was newly surprised by a divorce and exhausted from work, why it was that he continued to volunteer so much, serving on boards and on the vestry at church while he worked so many hours. Even as a young teenager, I could see the toll the deep fatigue was taking on him.

He responded by quoting those words from the Gospel of Luke that President Kennedy had borrowed as well: "For those to whom much is given, much is expected."

Both the demonstration of and espousal of service were key pieces of my makeup, and connecting with this value was important to staying strong and motivated in a job that I saw as discouraging, as possibly even unfair, and, in fleeting moments that seemed to be increasing in frequency, as deadening. By connecting to my core purpose, I could see that I was still serving. This validated the work I was doing and empowered me to act from a place of strength. I may not have been leading a flight platoon yet, but by connecting to my core purpose, I continued to see even the menial tasks as an opportunity to serve, full stop.

Understanding that my core purpose is to serve undergirds all of my subsequent work, informs much of how I spend my time out of uniform, and even more fundamentally, articulates a value that is a significant part of what makes me who I am. It sustains me when times are hard and gives me direction when I feel the need to course-correct. Drilling down to core purpose is fundamental to accessing and developing grit.

The Core Purpose Every Leader Shares

My first battalion commander, Lieutenant Colonel John Macdonald (later Major General Macdonald), promoted me from second lieutenant to first lieutenant on a nondescript fall day in a small, windowless room at the back of the battalion headquarters building at Simmons Army Airfield on Fort Bragg. My father was among the small group in attendance, as he had found a conference nearby to justify the long trip from my home state of Alaska. The battalion adjutant read the orders to the small gathering, and Lieutenant Colonel Macdonald and my father each pinned on a silver bar. Then Lieutenant Colonel Macdonald made a few remarks. The most memorable part of his comments was a short but weighty admonition: "The only good use of this promotion and the increased power that comes from it is the increased responsibility to take care of your people."

His wisdom came hard-earned from those who came before. General Maxwell Taylor is quoted as saying that "a reflective reading of history will show that no man ever rose to military greatness who could not convince his troops that he put them first, above all else."[5] General Melvin Zais summed it up in the title of his presentation at the United States Army War College: "You Must Care," the premise of which was so influential to management guru Tom Peters that he boxed up the text and gave it to four thousand midshipmen when he presented the inaugural Forrestal Lecture at the United States Naval Academy.[6]

I took Lieutenant Colonel Macdonald's words to heart. Caring for the people I led was the metric by which I weighed every decision as a platoon leader, as a company commander, and later as a manager in the corporate world as well. That prioritization never led me astray, though neither did it guarantee my success. I would recognize any failure in taking care of my people as the greatest I could make. But I'm ever grateful for those short words on that otherwise inconspicuous day. I learned through direction and action that leadership is a sacred trust.

This care for people is the standard of good leadership across all of the leaders interviewed for this book. "Mission first, people always," goes the Army mantra. Another less formal Army maxim states that, "There are no bad soldiers, only bad leaders." In the military, a leader holds her charge's lives in her hands, but the imperative to take care of and develop her people is just as clear for a leader in a corporation, nonprofit, and family, because it is—or should be—part of the core purpose for all who lead.

Over a decade later, when I was working at Microsoft, I remember looking for that core purpose more than once. During a particularly frustrating week, I asked my husband what good I was doing at this big technology company. He offered the original purpose of Microsoft's creators: to put a computer on every desk. That didn't do it for me. That connected neither to my head nor my heart. It was in the midst of interviewing for, accepting, and working through a difficult position where I had to turn over a long-standing team that I returned to that purpose. My purpose was to take care of the people on my core team. Each one of them was talented, each wanted to make a difference. Some weren't able to do their best work in the context of where the team was heading—ensuring that they found other opportunities was a difficult, sometimes painful, but ultimately rewarding task. Ensuring others had a chance to contribute and move toward their goals within our team's new direction, while taking care of the things that came up for them personally, was also rewarding. Sure, the team was operating more effectively and contributing more. But the heart of the undertaking was and always is about the people. Sometimes the most difficult circumstances are what bring out that connection to and appreciation of core purpose.

Every one of the leaders I talked to for this book has a special understanding of compassionate leadership, caring for the people they lead. But one in particular, Brigadier General Rebecca Halstead, shares a story that shows how easy it can be to lose sight of this understanding, particularly in the midst of a demanding deployment—and how hard she needed to work to be sure that she stayed connected.

At just five feet one, Rebecca Halstead had a tough time as a cadet at the United States Military Academy at West Point. "I wanted to quit every day," she says. But Halstead didn't quit, and decades later she pinned on her star, the first woman graduate of West Point to do so.

During Operation Iraqi Freedom, Brigadier General Halstead led the logistics effort and commanded twenty thousand soldiers whose role was to support a quarter of a million troops across Iraq. Her charges operated out of fifty-five different locations, conducting missions around the clock. Every day her soldiers moved millions of gallons of fuel and water, distributed tens of thousands of rounds of ammunition, ordered and tracked thousands of parts for fixing equipment, and more. There was no question that with so many moving parts, she had to be in contact with what was happening in the field. But with so many people extended over such a broad area, it was impossible for Halstead to be present at all times.

Halstead had several hundred people on her staff who were responsible for giving her efficient and accurate briefings, bringing together the data and helping her to see trends. Daily updates ran two hours, but with the tremendous spread of people and facilities across the theater, every minute was taken up in relaying data.

Within a couple of weeks Halstead recognized that something important was missing. The data was correct, the briefings efficient and to the point. But "they were already beginning to lose touch with the human dimension," she says.[7] "To me, they were failing to connect with the people on the ground who were doing the work or experiencing the chaos, conflict, and tragedy.

"It hit me square between the eyes during a morning update," she continues. "The briefer says, 'Ma'am, at 0315 hours this morning, there was a complex attack on one of our convoys.'"

The briefer gave a concise update including the unit, number of vehicles involved and people injured, and then moved on to the next slide without a moment's hesitation. Halstead stopped the briefing.

"I slammed my hand on the desk and said, 'Stop. What do you mean, next slide? Are you forgetting what the leadership on the ground must be dealing with based on this attack? For the wounded, lives are changed forever. Can you imagine the chaos that had to ensue while this was happening? How can we help the leaders dealing with this?'"

Halstead understood why details were being excluded, but deemed it unacceptable. There was so much to report, and so much for the staff to manage, that they were completely out of touch with the soldiers on the ground, the people who were doing the work, and feeling the consequences. This would inform the way Halstead led going forward. She couldn't send all her staff out to visit units, and that wasn't their job. She would have to make that choice herself.

At the same time, she needed to make the connection for the staff.

She turned to her command sergeant major, the senior noncommissioned officer in charge of soldiers, and gave him immediate direction.

"I want a digital photo of every commander—company, battalion, and brigade—and every first sergeant and command sergeant major. I want those photos hung on the walls of the operations center!"

It was not an easy task. Halstead and her command sergeant major were responsible for over two hundred company-sized units, twenty-seven battalions, and sixteen brigade-level headquarters. It was nearly five hundred photographs.

Over the next week the pictures began appearing on the walls. Halstead issued a simple requirement: "When a battle-loss report comes in from a unit, I want you to go to the wall and look at the leaders who are dealing with the situation."

Almost immediately, the command headquarters began to feel more cohesive. Halstead herself felt more connected, even on those days when she could not get out to visit a unit herself. Because she found a way to ensure that she and her staff reconnected to their ultimate mission, the staff began internalizing the human dimension more fully, and Halstead could make decisions based not only on data, but on her core purpose: taking care of her people.

While Halstead had to get creative about how she stayed in touch with her core purpose, Katie Higgins stumbled into direct contact with hers. Though she went on to become the first woman to fly with the Blue Angels, she isn't particularly interested in talking about that experience when we speak on the phone. Instead, she tells me about her deployments, and especially the one flying the C-130 gunship known as Harvest Hawk in support of ground troops in Afghanistan.

It was her first deployment as a young Marine. "I was part of the Harvest Hawk mission in Afghanistan, where we provided close air support for US forces," she says. "Being able to deploy to protect American lives was the best feeling in the world."

Harvest Hawk is a modification of the C-130J that Higgins was qualified to fly, and which was used for aerial refueling. The modification involved replacing the hose-refueling pod on the outboard wing with an M299 quad-mount Hellfire-missile launcher. Harvest Hawk also carries a dual launcher for Griffin missiles.

Code One magazine recounts the details of Higgins's mission itself: "The message received by the battalion watch officer in the operations center was as urgent as it was precise: 'Second platoon is in sustained contact. Ground commander is requesting Harvest Hawk for an immediate priority JTAR [Joint Tactical Air Request]. Advise estimated arrival time when able.'"[8]

The US Marines taking enemy fire in Afghanistan who sent that message weren't making a general request for close air support. They weren't trying to flag down a fighter in the area with a couple of bombs to spare, although any help would have been appreciated. What those ground troops wanted was one specific aircraft overhead to make their problem go away—and make it go away now.

Higgins was copilot on the mission.

"When we got the call to stand by for a nine-line [the briefing requesting an engagement], I was like: Hell yeah, it's on!" she remembers. "We could hear the rounds coming in on the radio, and then an RPG [rocket-propelled grenade]. It was definitely an adrenaline rush."

It was a daytime mission, but the cloud deck was at the orbiting altitude for her aircraft, so "we had to fly below our usual altitude, avoiding the mountains. It was a really dynamic situation. But when there are guys on the ground, well, failure is not an option."

She put two Hellfire missiles on the target, neutralizing the enemy and ensuring safety for the Marines on the ground.

"I was so excited to be able to do what I had been trained to do," she says.

A year later, she was in a bar on base when a guy walked up to her.

"Hey, you guys shot for us last year," he said. "I was in the platoon that was pinned down. I recognize your voice."

Coming face-to-face with her core purpose—saving the lives of her fellow Marines—"gave me chills," Higgins says. It was amazing, she continued, "Putting a face to those guys, having the opportunity to give people the chance to be alive." It's not every day that you get to look your core purpose in the eye, but when you do, it's a memory that lasts a lifetime, and an incredible motivator to stay the course.

Connecting Your Core Purpose to Your Story

As powerful and important as uncovering your core purpose is, it doesn't happen in a vacuum. Once you know your core purpose, you can see how it relates to the themes in your own story. Clarity in this foundational work can help guide you in your decisions.

Author and theologian Frederick Buechner once said that you find your vocation in the place where your deep gladness and the world's deep hunger meet. How and where you find that vocation may change over the years, but that is no reason to delay the pursuit. In a given situation or place in your life, you might ask yourself: What is most needed here? How can I be a part of making this happen? It doesn't have to be the decision for the rest of your life, but it can help you define your purpose where you are right now.

My work on this book came about because of a request for guidance from a lieutenant, and because of feeling an immediate responsibility—and joy—at the opportunity to give back to others who might need help navigating through circumstances like those that I had found so difficult. It was good knowing that my challenges might help others. In writing this book, and in the speaking and training that I do, I'm able to amplify lessons and stories that are needed by so many. It's a true privilege.

When I moved to a small community in Washington State with my family five years ago, I heard about and started to see the significant economic disparity representative of so many rural populations. The community was too small to have much if any scaffolding for its most vulnerable members. Opportunity was limited for many. What stood out most for me was the utter lack of public space for people of all backgrounds to be together for healthy civic engagement. The more I learned about the influence of such space on healthy communities, the more evident the opportunity seemed to be. Our local library, which had the square footage of a trailer, was housed in a building intended over a decade prior to be temporary. The library did not meet the needs of the current and growing community.

Building a new library had the potential to meet the needs of our elderly population, offering lifelong learning and places to come together. It would meet many of the requirements to support children in their education. It would provide broadband and other technology to those who did not have access to such things at home. In short, it would help level an uneven playing field, offering equal access to opportunity while bringing people of all backgrounds together. I had experience in operations, in marketing and sales. This was a place to contribute. I thought of my father's reminder, "To those to whom much is given, much is expected."

As of the writing of this book, we are nearly 80 percent of the way to funding the library through private donations combined with generous contributions from the state, and in partnership with the town and the district. It has required more from me than I could have imagined, but the core purpose of building community and working toward equalizing opportunity for all is what has driven me when things have been difficult. Drilling all the way down to my core purpose, I arrive again at service, the same thing that drove me over twenty years ago.

The reason I share this example is because there may be times when you find your core purpose in doing something outside of work. The connection to this core purpose in any sphere of your life will buttress you in other areas. Knowing your place in the world is important, full stop.

Finding your purpose may help you find your direction. It will also give you ballast to steady you as you face rough seas, as it did for General Ann Dunwoody.

In 2005, Dunwoody became the army's highest-ranking woman officer when she was promoted to lieutenant general and assigned as the Army's deputy chief of staff and head of logistics, a job that would take her to the Pentagon, across the Potomac River from Washington, DC. Although her career in the field had presented Dunwoody with plenty of resistance and challenge (she was one of the first women to complete the rigorous parachute rigger training, the first woman to command a battalion in the 82d Airborne Division, and the first woman at Fort Bragg to be promoted to the rank of general officer), it was the corridors of the Pentagon that General Dunwoody found the most fraught with difficulty.

The iconic building in Arlington, Virginia, that houses the Department of Defense has more offices than the Empire State Building. With places to eat, dry cleaners, coffee shops, gyms,

clothing stores, and flower shops on its grounds, it feels more like a small city than an office building. In fact, within the walls of the Pentagon are five separate zip codes that are each served by their own police force and department of motor vehicles.

The scale of the Pentagon and its unusual naming conventions—rooms are named by their ring, their corridor, and then their room numbers—can make the building confusing even for alumni to navigate. But despite its size, a person might run into the chairman of the Joint Chiefs in line for coffee. The august physicality of the building is indisputable, but the experience of working there—which a friend of mine describes as a blend of patriotism and professionalism—leaves the biggest impact. "You don't impress yourself on the Pentagon," my friend says. "The Pentagon impresses itself on you."

It certainly impressed itself on Dunwoody. When she was named chief of staff of logistics in October of 2005, she was tasked with providing guidance and oversight in logistics, sustainment, and maintenance for the entire US Army. It seemed to be a perfect place to leverage her experience with and knowledge of warfighter requirements, while staying connected to her core purpose of taking care of the soldiers in her charge. But the highest levels of government had their own rules, and figuring out how to work within them would challenge Dunwoody in ways she'd not yet known in previous assignments.

The hierarchy she encountered at the Pentagon consisted of three layers, each with its own intimidating nickname: At the top were the Three Kings, a trio of lieutenant generals (three stars) who made all the critical budget recommendations; then the Three Wise Men, a group of brigadier or major generals (one and two stars); and at the lowest rung, the Three Wise Guys, colonels who each had veto power over even those leaders with higher rank, including then Lieutenant General Dunwoody herself.

When she arrived, Dunwoody clearly saw that the Army needed to automate the system it used to manage its billions of

dollars of inventory. Without automation, company commanders could not realistically keep track of their equipment, and often couldn't get access to the materials they needed to fulfill their mission. But getting the Three Wise Guys, Three Wise Men, and Three Kings to approve her requests for the funds to implement this much needed automation was next to impossible.

When we connect by phone, she remarks that "the government bureaucracy was brutal and frightening in its ability to make it extremely hard to get anything done."

Yet Dunwoody didn't give up. She challenged the decisions of the Three Kings all the way to the chief of staff of the Army, and finally received the funding she needed.

Dunwoody stayed committed when things were tough by remaining connected to her core purpose, which was making a difference for the soldiers in her charge. Many senior military leaders become disconnected from leading soldiers as they move into staff positions, but by reminding herself of her original purpose, Dunwoody was able to shift gears and do the senior-level work she needed to do.

Dunwoody's core purpose was part and parcel of her story, and vice versa. "I never considered myself anything other than a soldier," she tells me. "Knowing that soldiers on the battlefield could not do their jobs as efficiently and effectively as they could with this equipment, and knowing the Army was wasting taxpayer dollars buying more stuff because it didn't have the tools to see what it had was a huge motivator," she says.

Knowing her own core purpose allowed her to focus the organization she led on *its* core purpose: getting the warfighters what they needed to do their work.

For General Dunwoody, the intersection of purpose (making a difference) and story (she was and always will be a soldier at heart) put her in the ideal position to push through challenges, navigate her way through uncharted and seemingly impossible

bureaucracy, and change the focus of the entire Army logistics organization. Whatever the nature of your challenge, uncovering your core purpose prepares your foundation for grit.

Whether enduring hallucinations in the dark of night, the frustrations of deadening work, or the recalcitrance of entrenched bureaucracy, when you do the work to uncover your core purpose, you prepare yourself for the times when you will most need grit.

Knowing your core purpose will also help you connect with others who either share that core purpose or are committed to helping you fulfill yours, which, as you'll see in the next chapter, is another critical component of grit.

EXERCISE

Unearth Your Core Purpose

1. Challenge yourself to spend quiet and focused time discerning your core purpose. Pick one aspect of your life you want to interrogate—it could be professional, or personal. Ask yourself why it is that you are doing what you're doing. That first answer is likely your purpose. Now ask it again, four more times, writing down your answer each time. How does your purpose differ from your core purpose? What core purpose does this questioning start to tease out?

2. Purpose comes from your head, but core purpose comes from your heart. To help deepen your understanding of core purpose, consider what it is, within the context of your work, that breaks your heart. At Microsoft, the functionality of my team did not break my heart (though I was still responsible for such functionality). Knowing people's stories, hopes, and

dreams did. That's how I connected to my core purpose. What breaks your heart? What does that tell you about your core purpose, and connecting your head to your heart?

3. Now consider how your core purpose, representing the desires of your heart, connects to your story. Where do you see your core purpose in your story? Take your lifeline exercise and look for where you see connections between the events you've identified and your core purpose.

Part Two

LEARN

— 3 —

Draw Your Circle

"Those friends thou hast, and their adoption tried,
grapple them to thy soul with hoops of steel."

—William Shakespeare

After six months of sleeping on a cot in a tent in Bosnia-Herzegovina and flying armed aerial-reconnaissance missions nearly every day, our battalion was ready to go home. As much as I loved the mission focus and the flying, it was a lonely time, too. For many of the warrant-officer pilots, it was yet another deployment, yet more time away from their families. One reported that he would be transferring to the Coast Guard once we returned—his wife had given him an ultimatum. He'd been gone too much, deployed too many times. On that final day, we flew north, a long and loose formation of twenty-four Apaches and eight Black Hawks, back through Slovenia, Hungary, and Austria, over the Alps, across the patterned farms and small clusters of villages, and landed in Germany. A week later, the helicopters were prepared for their transatlantic crossing by boat, and we were scheduled for the next available flight.

Redeployment came in fits and starts. The schedules for transport fluxed constantly. One minute we'd be told to muster, and hours later we'd be dismissed. By the time we boarded the plane, shuffling under the weight of fully loaded duffel bags on our backs, rucksacks on our fronts, and helmet bags over our shoulders, too many false starts had robbed us of excitement. The lengthy intercontinental flight, broken only by a short re-fuel stop at Ireland's Shannon Airport in the middle of the night, intensified our collective fatigue. In the seats around me, soldiers talked about the family they'd see, the wives they'd missed, their kids. I stared straight ahead and worked to ignore the emptiness. Then I closed my eyes and tried to sleep. I wasn't coming back to anyone. My parents lived on the other corner of the continent, in Alaska. I could only hope my old roommate had left my car in the hangar parking lot.

We landed at Pope Airfield on the north end of Fort Bragg in the middle of the night. Our battalion unloaded the plane, placid with exhaustion. Once down the steps and onto the tarmac, we waddled with our heavy bags in an untidy line toward the hangar, its bright lights piercing the darkness. Cheers issued from the direction of the hangar as we approached, and the shape emerged of a small crowd lining the ropes leading to the wide hangar doors. The relief and joy in the faces of those waiting and, on recognition, in those of the uniformed souls stumbling forward, made me smile, even as my own feeling of emptiness sank deeper. I walked forward, happy for my soldiers, for my pilots, for all those returning to families, while feeling more alone myself. I continued past them, toward my car.

It was then I heard my name. In the midst of the crowd, the faces of Dougald and Tori, a retired couple from St. John's Episcopal Church, which I attended, came into focus. I had met Dougald and Tori two years earlier, on my first Sunday at church in Fayetteville. Since then they had invited me over many times for home-cooked meals and conversation, a sporadic family life in the midst of the unfamiliar. They had called the rear-detachment headquarters a couple of times a day to find out when I'd be coming home. A rush of relief and gratitude overwhelmed me. I was home. I was wanted home. Their presence was proof that I was loved. All soldiers know it is the circle of community that pulls them through the very hardest times. Drawing the circle matters, and it matters a lot.

Why Your Circle Matters

There are two truths about your circle that are critical to your success. The first is that no one goes it alone. You have to have your team. That team might come from a number of different places—and it must include people from both inside and outside of work. When I was at Fort Bragg, Dougald and Tori were part of my team.

The second truth is that you can't be everyone's friend, and someone who doesn't support you might be someone you don't need in your circle. It's one of the harder lessons, but an important one.

That's why I use the image of drawing a circle—you want to know who's inside your circle and who's not (see figure 3-1). This isn't about playing favorites or being exclusive. It's about knowing from whom you will draw strength, and setting boundaries so that you don't spend your energy on relationships that aren't supportive. This is another critical aspect of grit, and one that you can proactively develop.

Developing your circle prepares you for circumstances that require grit. Even the Army recognizes the ability to build strong, trusting relationships as a key skill for resilience and a building block of strength.

Army Regulation (AR) 350-53 articulates the reason for the relationship-related dimension:

FIGURE 3–1

Your solar system of connections

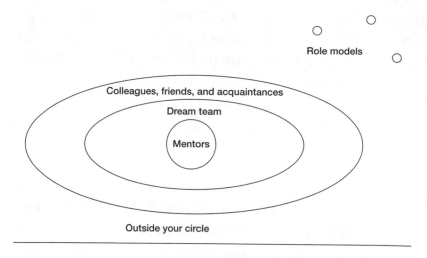

Developing and maintaining trusted, valued relationships and friendships that are personally fulfilling and foster good communication, including a comfortable exchange of ideas, views, and experiences. Adherence to the Army Values and other beliefs embodied in the Army profession and ethics help form and strengthen bonds of trust and esprit de corps that promote relationships and enhance resilience. These relationships are important because they serve as a support network for those who experience setbacks in life.

The importance of drawing the circle goes beyond emotional well-being. Dr. Moran Cerf, a neuroscientist at Northwestern University who studies decision making, finds that who you surround yourself with is one of the most important decisions you will make, because of its influence on your behavior and personality.

Cerf's research indicates that people make fewer decisions than they think they do, often—instead—using social cues even at a subconscious level to arrive at choices they might otherwise avoid. Proximity is a main contributor. When two people spend a lot of time together, their brain waves start to mirror each other.

As Cerf explained to *Business Insider,* "We see time and again that just being next to certain people actually aligns your brain with them based on their mannerisms, the smell of the room, the noise level, and many other factors. This means the people you hang out with actually have an impact on your engagement with reality beyond what you can explain."[1]

This kind of impact is no small thing, and underscores the reach of seemingly small decisions.

Not only do you want to be mindful of who is in your circle, you also want to be conscious of what role they'll play. Envision this like the orbits within the solar system. In the center is a mentor or mentors. The orbit nearest this center encompasses what I call your dream team, while everyone else in your circle is contained within the outermost orbit. Beyond that orbit are the people who are *not* in your circle, because those people have not proven themselves worthy of trust, are draining, or are simply not worth your energy or time. The shining stars you follow in the distance are your role models—the bright lights who inspire you from afar and encourage you to reach for greater heights. Let's start from the middle of this solar system of connections and work our way outward.

Every Leader Needs Mentors

Ideally, at the center of your solar system is a small team of trusted mentors. The leaders who have stayed the course, and who are featured in this book, often found that more than one mentor was important to their careers. It's also critical to know that mentorship is never a one-way street, but a relationship.

Anthony Tjan, author of *Good People*, identified five kinds of mentors with whom to consider cultivating relationships.[2] The first two kinds are those most often associated with mentorship: the master of your craft and the champion of your cause.

The first—the master of your craft—is the person you might think of as a traditional mentor, someone a few steps farther down the path than you who can advise, teach, inspire, and support you. This is a person to whom you can turn for insight and advice on strategic considerations and tactical skill development. In a 2007 study of diversity in the military, the officers interviewed who did not have mentoring relationships often had shorter careers than those who did, and those who had mentoring relationships were more often promoted to a higher rank, including that of general officer.[3] Just as important: this mentor may or may not be in your company or even necessarily your industry. The mentors in the diversity study didn't even need to be in the military to be effective—suggesting that it's more important to have someone knowledgeable in your corner than it is merely to have access to someone higher up the chain in your own realm.

The second in Tjan's list is someone who is the champion of your cause. While the first kind of mentor might be anywhere, this mentor or these mentors should be in your organization or your industry. These people are usually more senior, and they are active advocates on your behalf, and also helpful with connections in your industry.

(There are three other types of mentors on Tjan's list that are those members of your dream team. I'll cover this in the next section.)

Unfortunately, these first two critical relationships are likely to be unformed, as mentorship is on the decline, particularly for millennials. Research conducted by Harvard Business School found that most employees over forty could name a mentor, while only a few younger employees could.[4] It makes sense, as the intensified pressure to deliver that so many of us feel can easily prevent us from taking the time to seek—or become—a mentor. Yet mentorship is even more important for young women and young people: a 2015 study by a researcher at the Haas School of Business at the University of California found that female mentees with a high-status mentor enjoyed a greater rise in "legitimacy-enhancing signals"—in other words, their perceived status rose higher—than male mentees.[5]

That rise in status correlates to an increase in title and salary, too, as confirmed by an article published in the *Journal of Applied Psychology*. This meta-analysis looked at forty-three different studies and found that people with mentors earn more promotions and higher compensation than those without.[6] If that's not enticing enough, the researchers also found that mentees feel more satisfied with and committed to their careers. Notice that word, *committed*? That's grit.

In my conversations with the leaders I interviewed for this book, mentorship frequently came up as a topic that relates to grit—either because of its presence or notable absence. One of the best examples of the benefits of mentorship came from my conversations with Major General Dawn Dunlop.

In the middle of her career, Dunlop, a test pilot in every aircraft in the US Air Force inventory and a commander of the NATO Airborne Warning and Control System (AWACS) force, was selected as a White House fellow. In this prestigious nonpartisan leadership program founded in 1964 by President Lyndon Johnson, leaders work directly for top-ranking government officials and are paid as full-time government employees. White House fellows often go on to positions of leadership in both the military and civilian sectors.

During Dunlop's fellowship, she met Marsh Carter, who had been a White House fellow decades before and was one of the alumni who came to speak at the program when Dunlop was in attendance. Carter is a two-time Purple Heart recipient and Marine Corps officer who would later become the president and

CEO of State Street Bank and chairman of the New York Stock Exchange. He is passionate about flying—his grandfather had been the first professor of aerospace engineering at West Point— and Carter himself is a private pilot. Carter and Dunlop developed a friendship based on mutual respect and a love of flying, and began a mentoring relationship that Dunlop credits with major influence in her career.

"He always said that a woman working in a man's world needs a male mentor with daughters," she laughs.

Who exactly should you approach as a possible mentor?

"Someone who understands you, your work, and your style," says Christine Sandler, another mentee of Marsh Carter's who has served in a number of senior finance roles in New York for over three decades. In other words, someone with whom you resonate and who will seek to know you and help you develop as an individual.

Admiral Michelle Howard agrees. The first four-star African American woman in the Navy, Howard was always the first in her field. She couldn't find a mentor who looked like she did or would understand the specific challenges she faced. So Howard started seeking out other qualities in her mentors.

"It's about people who have the same purpose and motivations in life," she says. "What is it you want to accomplish? What attributes are you trying to gain in yourself? What do you see as the paragon of success in your field or in character? Go find the person who has those attributes."

While you can wait to find a mentor serendipitously, as Dunlop found Carter when he came to speak to the White House fellows, you don't have to delay. You might approach your HR department for suggestions, contact any professional organizations you're involved in, or reach out to the alumni office of your college or graduate program to see if they have formal mentor-mentee matching. Best of all is keeping your eyes open in your field, and observing the qualities of leaders around you. When you find someone from whom you would like to learn, approach that person respectfully.

Keep in mind that the mentor who will be good for you may not be an obvious choice. When Dunlop began her White House fellowship, she was assigned a woman mentor, another woman leader who had broken barriers in her field.

"The program thought that gender was what mattered," Dunlop says. "It absolutely was not."

Instead, Dunlop's relationship with Marsh Carter, formed on respect and shared interests, turned into the mentorship that would guide her career.

"Mentorship is situational, and it's personal," says Dunlop. "It's really more like a relationship. When I had questions, I asked him. When he had thoughts for me, he sent them. I might mention to him that I was going to work for someone new, and he would email back things he would consider when making a transition, or something he noticed when he looked at that person's experience. He would send articles or ideas I might not have come across. Sometimes he might ask for my thoughts on something he was about to present."

And that's a key thing to look for in a mentor—someone who isn't there only to instruct but also to ask, listen, and learn from you.

Dunlop credits the experience of being mentored by Carter with helping her help others.

"What I learned from Marsh helped me be a better mentor of women," she says.

How can you tell that a mentor is the right fit for you? Belle Rose Ragins, professor of management and specialist in mentoring at the Lubar School of Business at the University of Wisconsin, counsels seeking what she calls reciprocal mentorship. In this model, four areas of focus ensure a positive relationship. The first is mutual listening and affirmation. In other words, a mentoring session shouldn't feel like a lecture but a dialogue. Both parties in the relationship can maintain an open mind and be willing to learn from each other. The second characteristic is humility, which can be difficult for senior men. Yet a truly confident leader understands his own weaknesses, and uses his experiences, including his failures, as an opportunity for learning and example. Third is power sharing. Recognizing the innate privilege that comes with gender and race, mentors consciously work to put aside any power differentials within the context of the relationship and "are deliberate about sharing social capital, including influence, information, knowledge, and support with mentees." Finally, reciprocal mentorship is focused not only on career advancement and compensation but also on other areas of growth, including self-efficacy, resilience, and emotional intelligence. It's not just about getting ahead but about growth—personal and professional.

Christine Sandler recommends that someone looking to establish a relationship with a mentor set up ground rules from the beginning.

"Whether or not it's a formal program, you need to set up expectations," she says. "The mentee should come with specific tactical or strategic asks and have clear goals. The more specific a mentee can be, the better. That will help the mentor be prepared and thoughtful."

Take a moment to consider: is there someone in your life you can call a mentor, someone whose name you could write in the center spot in your solar system? If the answer is no, start to look for someone who might fill this vital role for you and help you navigate the path ahead.

Who's on Your Dream Team?

Take another look at figure 3-1. Let's expand now to the first circle of orbit beyond your core of mentors in your solar system: your dream team.

Whom do you invite into this circle? Both formal and informal relationships are important, and both social and professional. It's not where these ties come from that matter the most. It's the qualities of the people themselves. Moran Cerf's findings on the impact a leader's inner circle has on his or her performance suggests that people surround themselves with others who embody the traits they prefer. It follows that if you as a leader are preparing for tough times or expecting a high standard of performance, this circle should include people who support you and who teach or embody the traits you need to be successful. In other words, if you want grit, you've got to surround yourself with people who have it.

It's also important that the people on your dream team aren't all similar to you, whether of the same gender, cultural background, race, or profession. The importance of diversity in your dream team goes back at least to John Stuart Mill in the nineteenth century, when he wrote: "It is hardly possible to overrate the value of placing human beings in contact with persons dissimilar to themselves, and with modes of thought and action unlike those with which they are familiar. Such communication has always been, and is peculiarly in the present age, one of the primary sources of progress."[7]

Mill's wisdom is not lost on today's senior leaders. General Ann Dunwoody, the first woman to earn four stars in the Army, puts it plainly: "If you're sitting around the table with people who all look like you, and sound like you, you're going to have a narrow view of things."

While networks of women can be helpful to women leaders, it is important not to consider them sufficient. In their 2007 book, *Through the Labyrinth: The Truth about How Women Become Leaders*, Alice Eagly and Linda Carli specifically warn that even "in organizations that are more integrated by gender . . . networks are often largely segregated, with women joining other women and men with other men. All-women networks are limiting for women. Greater influence would follow from participating in the networks with the generally more powerful group of men."[8]

Just as you need different types of people, there are also different roles available in the cast of your dream team. This is where the last three types of mentors identified by Anthony Tjan come in.

The third relationship of Tjan's five is the copilot—a title most apt for this book, considering the number of aviation leaders included. This is someone who is a close friend at work, someone who fulfills the relationship aspect of purpose as described in chapter 2. This person is someone to whom you can vent when needed, and with whom you discuss navigating the complexities at work. This kind of relationship improves the quality of your work as well as your level of engagement. And this isn't limited to just one person—none of these roles are. You may, if you're lucky, have several people who fit in this category.

The next relationship is the anchor, and again, you may have more than one person who acts as an anchor for you. This might be a friend in your industry or not, and can also be a family member. This person listens, and helps you stay positive when things get tough. The relationship with this person is more holistic, so you will help each other in areas like setting and balancing priorities, staying focused on your core purpose, and staying connected to your values.

Finally, the reverse mentor. Tjan discusses the reverse mentor being central to the relational aspect of mentorship. Crucially, Tjan defines the reverse mentor as the person who teaches you as you mentor them—your mentee. (We will talk more about this in the next section.) Tjan comments that "talking to my mentees gives me the opportunity to collect feedback on my leadership style, engage with the younger generation, and keep my perspectives fresh and relevant."[9]

Be a Mentor

It's as important to be a mentor as it is to be a mentee. As Dawn Dunlop told me, "If we don't mentor younger women, they will not have the advantage of our experience." Research also suggests that leaders who take the time and make the investment to mentor others do better themselves.[10]

The benefits of stepping up to mentor, even if you don't feel like you are far enough along the path to be useful, are wide-ranging. There will always be someone coming up behind you who would benefit from your help.

"When you see talent, you have to be able to step in and make a difference," Dunlop says. "It doesn't take that much time, and you can change someone's life. That one person can go on to have multiple impacts on multiple people."

To be an effective mentor, challenge yourself to extend your circle. "If you're a male leader and you're having guys over for Scotch and cigars so that you can convey your lessons on leadership, you need to think about ways to make these opportunities more inclusive, or you are disadvantaging all those who can't attend," Dunlop says.

Air Force F-16 fighter pilot "Lucky" Heather Penney is an aviator through and through. Now retired from the Air National Guard, she can still be found racing planes as a civilian in Nevada. But Penney's early years in the Air Guard were far from smooth. She reflects at length on the difficulties, and how having a mentor made all the difference for her.

"Everyone says pilot training is going to be the best year of your life and it's true," she says. "I absolutely loved it. But it was also really hard, and not just because of the rigors of academics and flying. I was the only girl in my class, and I didn't really fit in with the machismo, even though I tried, and I didn't have any female role models to look up to and emulate. There was a female instructor pilot in another flight class, but even though she was great with the guys, she was cold to me and barely even acknowledged my existence. She was widely regarded as one of the best instructors in the wing, and so her guidance and mentorship would have been so valuable. It was really intimidating and discouraging, and it wasn't helpful in figuring out the group dynamics. I've often said that the jet doesn't care if you're a man or a woman, it just cares how well you fly. But the truth of the matter is that the squadron is made of people, and group dynamics matter. I had a great bunch of guys in my class, and it was still awkward to negotiate.

"But there was one other girl, Christine Callahan, who was a couple of classes ahead of me. Grinder [Christine's call sign] was so friendly and supportive, it was a really important lesson on how critical mentorship is," Penney says. "Grinder was transformative for me. I knew that if I ever saw another girl coming behind me it was my obligation to look out for her and others. The connection to another woman helped me understand that I was not alone."

Christine Callahan wasn't just a leader during flight training—she went on to become the first female F-35 pilot and remains a friend to Penney and an inspirational role model to all young women. Today she is a civilian flight instructor for the F-35.

Penney's hard-earned understanding of the importance and responsibility of paying mentorship forward is a crucial point. As soon as you have even a little bit of experience under your belt, understand that you are a role model for others, and look for ways to help mentor others, to complete the circle. Not only will you be helping others navigate what you've already mastered, but you'll do better in your own career, too. It's the best kind of win-win.

Once You Have Your Dream Team, Be Open Enough to Ask for Input

There are many functions of a dream team: Camaraderie is encouraging. It's important to process challenges and information with others you respect and trust. Being around smart people promotes better decision-making skills. But one of the greatest advantages of gathering a dream team is also the easiest to neglect: asking for help, and then accepting that guidance.

Angel Hughes learned how important it was to lean on her dream team at a critical time. Daughter to Haitian immigrants in New Jersey, Hughes had fallen in love with astronomy from a young age, and began studying to be a pilot in high school. She went the civilian route first, earning her Certified Flight Instructor and Certified Flight Instrument Instructor ratings. The economy was weak, though, and pilot jobs were hard to come by. Hughes looked into military options, and decided on the Coast Guard for its mission and quality of life. She headed to flight school, conducted with the Navy. Despite her extensive aviation knowledge from the civilian sector, Navy flight school did not go smoothly.

"The six weeks of Navy aviation ground school was like my four-year degree compressed into six weeks," Hughes says. "Most of my classmates were Coast Guard, Navy, and Air Force Academy graduates with engineering degrees."

She felt lost.

"At one point, I thought I was going to wash out. I had this fear of failure, but did not believe failure was an option. I was one test away from failing out. I confided in a friend, and she asked for help on my behalf. Suddenly I started getting calls from people I didn't even know."

Hughes had to learn to ask for help. Because she was willing to reach out, she pushed through ground school successfully. Then she was back in the air, and back in her element again.

Getting through that experience set her up for continued success, and she became an aircraft commander in Mobile, Alabama, the only woman—and woman of color—flying search-and-rescue missions.

One piece of advice I was given early on was to find two people whom I could trust as advisors and otherwise keep things close to the chest. Despite my inexperience and inability to fully realize that advice, I did practice the skill of asking for input, from people both junior and senior to me. I went to them only after I had exhausted my own learning first, so that they knew the work had been done. Going to someone for help never replaces hard work, and in fact the courage to reach out should come from knowing you have used every resource you can on your own before asking for assistance. Asking requires vulnerability, but it always pays off.

The luckiest a new platoon leader might be is to have an excellent platoon sergeant. In my first platoon, I had the best: Sergeant First Class (SFC) Couturier. We all called him C, the first letter of his last name. He pushed back when he didn't agree, but he always disagreed behind closed doors. If I stuck to my decision, he marched out of my office and gave directions to the platoon as though it were his idea. He embodied what Amazon CEO Jeff Bezos has termed "disagree and commit,"[11] and C's example was one of the biggest gifts to me as a young leader. C let me know how the soldiers I didn't know as well were doing, and told me how best to take care of them, either by recognition or discipline appropriate to the requirement. He stood up for me and for our platoon, and represented us all with stellar professionalism. C made it easy to ask for his advice.

My second platoon sergeant was the opposite. I'd led my first platoon for a year when our sister battalion was selected to deploy to Bosnia, and I requested a transfer to take a platoon in the deploying battalion. It was an exciting opportunity, but it also meant I lost the relationship with my first platoon sergeant that had helped develop my own leadership. Fortunately, C had helped me understand the standard of performance I could and should require. When pushed to disciplinary action with my second platoon sergeant, I sought the counsel of our battalion command sergeant major. It was necessary to have the support of the ranking noncommissioned officer in any disciplinary action taken against a sergeant first class, and I valued—and needed—the command sergeant major's advice, but I had to have the humility and confidence to ask for it. It was a difficult situation, and the command sergeant major didn't pretend otherwise, but I'd done my work before coming to him, and he helped us move forward.

Asking for advice and looking for help can feel uncomfortable for leaders, whether it's because you're just starting out and still proving yourself, or because you've been around the block a few times and worry that it will undermine the respect you've worked so hard to earn. Your dream team gives you a safer place to get the support you need. Nearly every leader I interviewed for this book is quick to say that "no one does it alone." Trying to do it all yourself is not only stressful—it is also unsustainable.

The Outer Ring

As important as mentors and your dream team are, they are not the only relationships that matter. This is good news, because sometimes you'll find yourself in a situation where it feels like there is no one close by to fill those roles. That's where I found myself when, after returning from Bosnia and attending the captain's career course for training in military intelligence, I was sent to Korea. My first job was as logistics officer for the Apache battalion, before I took command of A Company, 1st Aviation Battalion, 2nd Infantry Division. As in the case of my platoons, I was the company's first female commander, and in part because of that, the camaraderie I had hoped for was tenuous at best.

I took responsibility for my part in addressing this situation. I would have to make an extra effort to reach out myself. One particularly memorable attempt at connection happened early in my command: I had overheard plans a group of my peers and senior warrant officer pilots were making to gather in a fellow commander's apartment. I decided, despite my discomfort, to stop by, trying to act nonchalant.

When I arrived and knocked at the door, somebody yelled "Come in!" and I walked inside. All of my fellow commanders were in the room and at least one more senior officer, as well as a number of the battalion's senior warrants, all drinking beer and oriented toward the television in the corner of the room. A few faces turned and started to smile, but then turned nervously back to the television. They weren't working to exclude me, but it took only a moment to figure out the source of their discomfort. A hard-core pornography video played on the screen around which the group was oriented. I hesitated briefly, and then stammered an excuse that couldn't have been casual if I'd tried.

"Guess I'll see you guys later," I said, and walked out.

Forming strong relationships with those around me in this environment was near impossible. There were nights when a group of us would sit around the grill with a beer or mixed drink after time in the gym, but experiences like these showed that the limitations were real, and came with additional baggage.

Then one day one of my soldiers didn't show up for morning formation. I was flying nights at that time, which meant that my duty day didn't start until the afternoon. When my first sergeant called me first thing in the morning, I knew it was bad news. Technically, the right thing to do would have been to report the missing soldier immediately, but the first sergeant urged a short and quiet investigation first.

The only way to get information on anything outside the confines of our base was to talk to a local, so I went to talk to

Mr. Park, who ran the cultural center on our small installation. I had taken a few classes with Mr. Park to learn a little bit of Hangul when I'd first arrived, and we had always had a good rapport. The first sergeant knew that the missing soldier liked a girl who worked at a bar a short walk from the security gate. Mr. Park headed out to talk to the bar's owner. We found the soldier at the girl's apartment, in violation of all of the security regulations under which our battalion—and, in fact, the entire 2nd Infantry Division—operated.

This was my first experience with a soldier running afoul of the Uniform Code of Military Justice. He was also one of my best soldiers. I needed advice.

I called a fellow commander with more experience in the position—one of those who'd been at the aforementioned apartment gathering—and although we were cordial, we were not friends. Again, reaching out wasn't easy. I knew that as the first woman to hold command in our battalion, I was constantly scrutinized and constantly judged. I didn't want to appear weak or unknowing, but I needed his input. Our communication was professional, and it was helpful. I assigned the soldier maximum extra duty, and he was demoted from corporal to specialist, but we avoided the more severe repercussions that would have happened by going up the chain of command.

Three relationships were critical in solving this challenge—the relationship with my first sergeant, the relationship with Mr. Park, and the relationship with my fellow commander. None were social, but all were respectful. While my previous efforts to establish a relationship with the commander did not result in friendship, they did result in a collegial interaction that facilitated the advice I needed.

You, too, may find yourself in a less-than-ideal situation for developing substantive relationships; perhaps because you're in the minority, or you just don't feel you fit in to the workplace culture. Developing at least a few respectful relationships—even if they aren't particularly close—will help deepen your grit factor by giving you the support that you may need. These people may not be on your dream team, but they still matter.

This is the outer ring. This part of your team might come from anywhere. It's a reminder of the importance of keeping as many of your interactions on good terms as possible and helping out wherever you can, assuming you are able to stay connected to your values, your purpose, and your mission.

Deciding Who's outside the Circle

Drawing a circle means that some people are in, and others are out. The challenges of developing community require careful choices, and yet some women leaders have a hard time overcoming the idea that they don't have to please everyone.

Naval aviator Karen Brasch counsels that "Respect is more important than being liked. It takes a long time to earn and a second to lose it. I remember a commander calling me into his office. He told me 'Everyone likes you, but what will you do if they don't? You need to know that not everyone is going to like you . . . and that's OK.' I decided I would rather be respected for what I knew than liked for any other reason." Lieutenant Commander Krysten Ellis agrees. After her frustrations with perceptions in the fleet, she reminds leaders: "You don't have to be everyone's best friend."

For Sarah Burrow, the first woman to fly in the US Marine Corps, the lessons of the importance of building her team came from enduring the betrayal of those she thought supported her.

When Burrow joined the Marines, she didn't expect to fly—women still weren't allowed. As the daughter of a Marine and as a Midwestern farm girl from outside Toledo, Ohio, she had always known she wanted to wear the uniform. Her father had not encouraged it.

"He was a Marine in the fifties, when people still died in boot camp," Burrow says, "but I'd always wanted to join."

She completed officers basic school at Quantico, Virginia, requested aviation maintenance, and was assigned to aircraft-control school.

"I was halfway through aircraft-control school when Secretary of Defense Les Aspin lifted the flight restrictions on women," Burrow remembers, referring to the lifting of combat exclusion in the spring of 1993. She read about it in the newspaper, and holding the article in her hand, she called Marine headquarters to say, "This is what I want to do." Relaying this story, she assesses: "I can't imagine what that colonel must have thought about a little second lieutenant calling up and telling him she'd read something in the newspaper."

Burrow's timing was perfect. She was given a lateral transfer and arrived in Pensacola, Florida, for training. Pensacola is the westernmost city in the Florida panhandle, known for its stretches of beautiful white-sand beaches along Florida's emerald coast. It is also known as the cradle of Naval aviation, as Naval Air Station Pensacola was the first Naval air station in the country. She was a long way from her Ohio home.

Burrow did not find others as exuberant as she was about her arrival. What should have been the best year of her life turned miserable.

"It sucked," she says of arriving at flight school. "I was a loner. I had to be. People who had been my friends at basic were no longer my friends. There was a small group of us that had gone on weekend trips together, celebrated birthdays together. I saw one of them when I arrived at Pensacola, and said 'Hey! Let's go do something!'"

Burrow's friend looked at her and said, "I can't."

When she asked why, he said, "It wouldn't be right."

She never talked to him again.

"It was a really hurtful time," she says.

Finding her Marine friends falling away during flight training, Burrow developed important friendships with two women from the Navy who were also going through pilot training. She met her husband at flight school as well. But the betrayal of these friends would stay with her. Her suggestion to new leaders? "Know who your friends are."

In other words, know that some people will not make it inside any of the rings of your circle, and that's OK. You may wish they did, and it may be painful that they don't, but at least knowing that you have a place to move these people—outside of your circle—will help you stay focused on the people who belong inside.

If there is someone personally or professionally who is not supportive of you and your hard work, or who doesn't believe in you, that person doesn't deserve to be in your circle. More than that, it's important that you not waste valuable energy on those who will detract from values, from core purpose, and from mission. It's wise to be cautious and selective in populating your circle, too. Coming from more amicable and less competitive environments, it's easy to assume everyone is a friend, and it's a hard reality to discover otherwise. Here is hard-earned advice: Ignore the naysayers—absolutely shut them out. There are many who will not be willing to do the work, and those people will be the first to criticize and undermine your endeavors. In an effort to deflect from their own deficiencies, they may even work to undermine you personally. Stay focused on the task at hand. Take the high road, and stay positive. Be someone who can be trusted, and your circle will evolve with the kind of quality people you can support and who support you.

So Far, but Yet So Close: The Importance of Role Models

Several of the leaders I interviewed noted that they had people whom they emulated but who were not mentors or even, in some cases, people with whom they had relationships. In many cases, leaders followed an example in their families. In several cases, however, these role models came through media or external sources. These are the far stars in your solar system, lights you can observe and emulate even if they aren't in your circle.

These role models may be fictional characters as well, which emphasizes the importance not only of understanding your own story (as I covered in chapter 1) but of connecting to other stories that show examples, whatever their source. Lieutenant General Nadja West—the first woman of color to serve as Surgeon General of the Army and earn the rank of three stars—mentions both Uhura and Spock, from *Star Trek*, as role models—Uhura for her example as a black woman on the bridge of the Starship *Enterprise*, showing competence and rapport, and Spock for embodying the scientific mindset that ultimately motivated West to attend medical school and earn her doctorate.

Angel Hughes, the Coast Guard pilot we met earlier, found her inspiration in Bessie Coleman, the first African American (and Native American) woman pilot in the United States. Coleman had to travel to France to earn her wings, but she wouldn't let anything stop her. Hughes has paid back the inspiration, too, understanding its importance. She and commercial pilot Nia Wordlaw founded Sisters of the Skies with a stated mission to cultivate and promote minority women in the industry through scholarship, mentorship, and emotional support.

I remember looking for role models and finding excellent examples of leadership, but no women. Remember—the internet wasn't a thing back then. Examples were out there, but they were hard to find. Wherever you can find the story of another remarkable woman that draws you in, whether from real life or from the pages of a book, take inspiration. What made her successful? How did she navigate challenge? How did she rise up again after failure? During the interviews I conducted for this book, I found myself drawing strength from the stories of these remarkable women in a way that helps me understand my own experience better, even in retrospect. I hope you are drawing similar strength and understanding from the examples in these pages.

Role models set an example of what is possible and demonstrate how challenges can be overcome more universally. You can also learn specific skills from observing, reading about, and then modeling your approach after that of other leaders. Reading memoirs or biographies (even fiction), listening to interviews, and attending lectures are all ways to be introduced to people who may act as virtual support for you in the examples they set with their own lives.

It was the powerful women who authored the books Dougald and Tori gave me who became my role models in their own ways: Beryl Markham, in *West with the Night,* and Jill Ker Conway, in *The Road from Coorain.* Their lives showed focus and purpose, an insistence on making a difference despite social resistance, and a fierce commitment to their core purposes—aviation and education, respectively—despite the odds. With a penchant for adventure, for exploring continents and ideas, and with a disregard for the chorus of naysayers and defenders of the status quo, these two women refused to be held back. Beryl and Jill are people I'd love to know, and I like to think I do know them, if just a little, by spending time with their words. They continue to inspire and teach me.

When Relationships Are in Short Supply

Despite your best efforts at finding them, sometimes worthy candidates for your dream team may seem nonexistent, as was the case for Krysten Ellis when she joined the Navy and women were not yet allowed to earn their dolphins, the coveted submariner qualification. (The insignia worn by American submariners shows two dolphins on either side of a submarine—an image representing both the special historical understanding of dolphins as attendant to sailors, and the way that dolphins dive and surface again.)

The daughter of a submariner, Ellis grew up with a strong affinity for the Navy. She remembers sending her father twenty-five-word messages by telegram when he was deployed. After graduating magna cum laude with a degree in civil engineering from Auburn University, Ellis trained as a supply officer and was teaching reactor principles and mathematics at the Nuclear Power School when, in February 2010, Defense Secretary Robert Gates notified Congress of the Navy's intent to lift the ban on women in submarines. She immediately applied for the Women in Submarines program. The first women reported to submarine duty the following fall, Ellis among them.

Throughout her tours, Ellis built strong bonds with the sailors in her crews, regardless of their gender. She loved the work, but was frustrated with the challenges posed by being a woman.

"I had a good friend in one of the guys on board, and people started talking about what they thought was happening between us when there was nothing to talk about," she says. "It's frustrating, but I had to hold him at arm's length to manage perceptions. Either you manage misperceptions and rumors directly, or you have to keep things at arm's length. It's not fair, but it's reality.

"Another time, I called a senior enlisted guy on my team to pass along information he needed to know, and his wife was upset. He thought maybe if his wife met me, it would be better, so we arranged to meet at the food court in a mall, all three of us. It wasn't better. She started to scream at me in a public place."

The challenges that Ellis experienced—demeaning assumptions and accusations that interfered with the ability to nurture professional relationships—were similar to those faced at one time or another by many, if not most, of the leaders I interviewed for this book. Several women described a deep loneliness in their experiences, something I related to as well. This difficulty is exacerbated by the disconnect such leaders feel from the camaraderie they had hoped for or expected, and that they may observe among their coworkers. For all leaders, but especially for those whose work lives are lonely, strong social connections outside of work are paramount.

Most of my early assignments were incredibly insular—because of work requirements and geographical locations—but my last assignment, at Fort Bliss, Texas, was the opposite. Despite deploying for exercises around the world every other month, I put strict boundaries on my time when I was back in country. This was made easier by the fact that I'd decided to leave the military, but I still took pride both in my work and in the important task of leading my team. I was the most junior officer in the headquarters where I was assigned, so I sought out opportunity for social interaction outside of work, primarily by doing volunteer work and pursuing athletic interests. I joined a local choral group, volunteered as a Big Sister for a local teenager, attended church off base, and joined a group of triathletes. I trained with the triathletes every weekend that I was in town and swam each morning with the masters swim team at the University of Texas at El Paso. I still count some of that group among my friends two decades later. Every strong, supportive relationship you can build counts, and adds to your own grit factor.

Making the Time to Nurture Your Circle

Whether it was because of social exclusion by the majority, the requirements of managing perceptions, or other challenges within the professional realm, I rarely found building a professional community straightforward. In the midst of a given experience, I wasn't able to explicate the nuances of what would now be described as a challenge of intersectionality. My perception of the requirement to separate personal relationships completely from work also seemed to compromise forming a dream team.

Finding these relationships is tricky enough, but in the midst of onerous work challenges, finding the time needed for nurturing them is trickier still. Developing connections outside of work takes time, and time is something few of us have at any stage in our careers, but especially after one has ascended to a leadership role. As a young lieutenant, my work days often stretched to twelve hours or more, and six-day work weeks were not uncommon. Field-training exercises required extended periods away; deployments even more so. Developing relationships outside of work with this kind of a schedule is challenging at best. I think of time commitments more now that I'm older. The twelve-to-sixteen-hour days are still there, though now that time is taken up with a combination of work and family requirements. As grateful as I am for all that fills my life, I know, as we all do, that there is simply not a lot of flex time.

Prioritizing the development of those relationships outside of work is the first step. Maintaining them is the second, and just as important. This maintenance is something that can easily be overlooked until it's too late. Submariner Krysten Ellis shared one of her hardest lessons from her service.

"I was forward deployed for thirteen months and struggled to maintain relationships, resulting in a very solitary life for a while," she says. "My husband and I, dual military, grew apart and separated when I came home. Even my closest family became somewhat estranged after the complications of keeping in touch.

"It was very difficult to wake up one day and realize how profoundly alone I felt, and it took months and years to build many of those ties anew. It wasn't my fault, it wasn't their fault . . . but relationships are a two-way street, until you deploy. At that point, you have to make it your responsibility and understand that if you don't, everything and everyone back home will be completely foreign when you return. Everyone needs a strong support structure, and now I know that I must work extra hard to maintain it . . . not just for them, but for me as well."

Ellis is candid about a challenge many leaders face. In the midst of incredible demands on your time and energy, how is it that you can find time to nurture relationships? The reality is that you can't afford not to. That means working to develop opportunities to connect, reaching out and putting dates on the calendar. Many women I've talked to have found incredible value in joining a women's leadership group. It may mean asking about the high-potential group in your organization. It may mean looking for relevant professional conferences and making a point to attend them. It is just as important to prioritize your family time, your time with friends, and fit vacations into your schedule. If you struggle to do this, consider what it is you'll regret in five or ten years. You may want to put boundaries on work if necessary to ensure you spend time with people and prioritize personal events as well as professional requirements.

No matter how demanding or technical the mission, the key to success in any endeavor is always all about people. Superior performance and follow-through are the base line. Success follows with relationships that support this work, and attention to those relationships should be as big a part of your focus as anything else you do.

EXERCISE

Draw Your Circle

1. Draw your solar system, with a center point (your mentors), and an orbit beyond that (your dream team). Who is in the

center point? The first orbit? Who should be outside of your circle?

2. Whom do you consider to be role models, whether you have ever met them in real life or not? Give each of these folks their own star outside your solar system.

3. Who would you like to have in your circle who is not there already? How can you cultivate those relationships?

4. What first step might you take to connect to a possible new mentor? Can you set up a meeting? Invite the person to coffee?

5. What are you doing to sustain and build the relationships you already have? How can you carve out more time for nourishing relationships at every level of your solar system? Some leaders ensure they are home for dinner and then get back online to finish work after the kids are in bed. Some leaders draw strict boundaries around their weekend time. Consider what will work in your circumstances to prioritize relationships at home and at work.

6. Who might you mentor? Who can you sponsor? How can you use your experiences to give back to others working their way up at lower levels?

— 4 —

Listen Like a Leader

"When people talk, listen completely.
Most people never listen."

—Ernest Hemingway

S immons Army Airfield sits on the edge of Fort Bragg in central North Carolina, in a part of the state known as the Carolina Sandhills. I remember the tall, long-needled pines and the air sticky with moisture from spring to fall. I signed in to the headquarters of the 229th Attack Aviation Regiment in the late spring of 1995, newly trained to fly the Apache helicopter, and was assigned to 3rd Battalion to work in the operations shop. Unspoken, but lost on nobody, was that my arrival marked the very first integration of a woman attack pilot into the 229th—the only one out of 120 pilots.

After a frustrating year in the operations shop with minimal flying, I earned my way to platoon leader in the A Company Aces. The company shared a painted brick wall with the operations shop upstairs in the hangar, through which I heard the commander screaming regularly at the lieutenant whose platoon I was slated to take over when he finished his assignment. Though I'd had a chance to get to know and understand the value of different parts of the battalion during my time in operations, every lieutenant knows that line positions matter most. I also knew that everything I did as a platoon leader would be scrutinized more than anything any of my male counterparts did. In retrospect, I don't know which was more motivating: the fear of failure or the commitment to succeed. Either way, I was determined to exceed the standards.

An aviation platoon leader in the 229th back then was responsible for four Apache helicopters, and for the pilots and crew chiefs who flew and maintained them. I was also responsible for my individual duties as a pilot and platoon leader. Leading my platoon included fulfilling my own tactical flight and mission requirements, as well as leading and evaluating the pilots in the platoon. I would learn quickly that though the demands of the airframe and the mission were significant, the real challenge lay outside the cockpit.

At the time, the officer-evaluation reports conducted annually for every commissioned and warrant officer were so inflated that in order to remain competitive we all had to earn top marks in every category. One of the sections included a rating on written communication. It occurred to me that we didn't actually assess or develop that skill, and that my background as an English major could come in handy. To address this oversight, I assigned every warrant-officer pilot in my platoon a book report to write, on any aviation-related book in which he had an interest.

I can see experienced leaders reading this and cringing, and looking back, I do too. One warrant officer requested a meeting, closed the door, and screamed his refusal to comply with such a ridiculous requirement. My heart raced. I worked very hard to remain calm in the face of the first direct opposition to my authority. I paused, and then explained that he could certainly make that choice, but that the result of his choice would be a lower ranking on his evaluation. His face turned so red I was worried he'd break a blood vessel.

Later that afternoon, a senior warrant officer from another company came to see me.

"Let's take a walk, lieutenant," he said. It was less an invitation than a command.

We walked down the hangar stairs and along the side of one of the Apaches opened up for maintenance and stood facing each other on either side of the helicopter's tail boom. I'd later hear this called tail-boom counseling. It was an excellent place to have someone tell you how much you've screwed something up, as the sound of the ass-chewing was masked by auxiliary power units whirring and metal carts squeaking across a noisy concrete floor.

"Listen, LT," he said. "You can make your pilots do these reports. It's within your power."

I felt momentarily validated and triumphant.

"But if you do that, they will do only what it is that you ask them to do and nothing else," he said. "You don't know all that goes into running this platoon. You can't succeed without them."

My elation evaporated, replaced by a growing embarrassment. I continued to listen, chastened.

"These guys are pilots," he said. "They joined the Army to be pilots, and they're good at it. They'll do anything you want them to do as pilots."

"Thank you," I managed to squeak, trying to sound in control. I headed back upstairs to my desk in the company room.

My choice wasn't really a choice at all. I had come into my position thinking about my own performance. I was so focused on doing the best job possible that I hadn't taken the time to listen to the people who had already been there. I hadn't worked to understand them. I hadn't understood how much my performance was tied to theirs. I was naive, myopic, and selfish. I tried to maintain a modicum of dignity as I revoked the book-report assignment.

I learned an important lesson that day: leaders need to listen first.

The importance of listening as a leader came up in nearly every one of the interviews I conducted with general officers for this book, and is supported by numerous outside studies as well. Whether it is listening up (to your boss, board, or member of your C-suite) so that you understand and can meet requirements, or listening laterally and down (to your colleagues, direct reports, and support staff) to understand the environment and how best to take care of your people, being a strong leader requires listening until it hurts. Of course, by itself, listening does not solve anything. Listening, and the information that comes from it, informs action. Without listening, you are setting yourself up for failure and perhaps embarrassment, as I learned in the hangar that day.

What does listening have to do with grit? A lot, it turns out. So much, in fact, that listening is a part of the US Army Master Resilience training. For leaders navigating challenging environments, actively listening helps you understand the environment and provides critical clues about how to proceed. Whether learning what is expected of you, or understanding how you can best take care of and develop your people, listening is a key component in giving you the information you need to make it through even the most difficult times. It gives you a tool you can use again and again, helping you begin effectively, ensuring you stay on track, and, as my story shows, helping you course-correct after a misstep.

Knowing how to listen will help you gather vital information and establish a trusting relationship with both coworkers and superiors, especially as the corporate world continues to shift away from top-down directive leadership. Today, leaders are expected to develop and employ the strengths of each team member, so it is more important than ever to truly understand the people who are working for you. To do that requires listening. The Army's maxim "mission first, people always" reflects the reasoning behind this work. In addition to stressing the right priorities, it is also the way the work gets done: you take care of your people, and they take care of the mission. That's not to say that there isn't tough love along the way—there always is. But it's very hard to support people personally and professionally if you don't know them, and hard to know them if you don't listen.

It's clear to me now that active listening is both the most underappreciated and most critical skill a leader can develop. The good news is that listening is a learnable skill. Learning to listen is part of setting the conditions for grit.

Listening Helps You Understand

Listening is a vital component of something every leader needs: understanding. I grew up with a calligraphic rendering of the prayer of Saint Francis on the wall outside our kitchen. One line of the prayer reads, "Lord, grant that I may not so much seek to be understood as to understand." Saint Francis knew that listening is an essential precursor to understanding. It's caring enough about others that you're willing to suspend your own desire to jump to judgment and consider that there may be other important perspectives. It does not necessarily mean that what you hear should inform direction or decision. The act of listening itself is important in the process of determining the best way to go forward.

One of the leaders I talked to who was smart enough to figure out how to listen from her first days in uniform describes, with characteristic humor, where her listening made all the difference.

As a major (a young field-grade officer), Dee McWilliams was one of only a small number of officers who had completed residential Command and Staff training at Fort Leavenworth—an achievement that was supposed to guarantee a coveted command slot. She headed to Fort Lewis, Washington (now Joint Base Lewis-McChord), to assume her command. On arrival, McWilliams was told that the colonel had just filled the command position she had been promised, and she was put instead into a staff position in planning. Despite her frustration and disappointment, McWilliams kept her wits about her enough to learn how to make the most of her assignment.

Soon after beginning her new position, McWilliams accompanied her boss to give a briefing to General Norman Schwarzkopf.

General Schwarzkopf was both revered and feared. His unofficial nickname was "Stormin' Norman," a moniker that would make its way onto a ski trail at Telluride and was indicative of his temper. Paired with his formidable size, this made interaction with him range from intimidating to terrifying. In his office, he had a sign hanging above the door that read: "When you dance with the bear, you quit when he's ready."

McWilliams's boss "was a face-time guy," she says. "But partway into his presentation, Schwarzkopf cut him off and dismissed him."

Face time with the general was in short supply. Being cut off was not altogether unusual, but it was no less mortifying.

A day before the next briefing to Schwarzkopf, her boss came to her and told her she would do the briefing. "I wasn't a briefer," she says. "But I figured I could do it." When they walked into the room, Schwarzkopf was looking down at his desk, engrossed in his work.

"I said 'Good morning, sir,'" she remembers.

Schwarzkopf's head snapped up.

"He had this surprised look on his face, and I could tell it took him a moment to process that he was being addressed by a woman."

McWilliams delivered her briefing, and just as she finished,

Schwarzkopf took his pencil and hurled it at her. It went right by her ear. She didn't flinch.

"What idiot at the Pentagon created this system?" he yelled.

McWilliams wasn't rattled. She had done her homework, and she knew that Schwarzkopf himself had built the system he was criticizing. She didn't allow herself to worry about how scared or embarrassed she might be. She listened, and listening gave her the opportunity and the objectivity to hear what Schwarzkopf was conveying beyond his words.

"I realized he was being funny," she says. "No one else in the room understood it, but he was being funny."

Taking the cue that humor was a valued mode of communication for the general, McWilliams leaned over and said quietly, "Sir, this ain't the 82nd [a unit at Fort Bragg in which Schwarzkopf had served]."

"I know," Schwarzkopf said. "Don't remind me."

A few months after her first briefing, she again accompanied her boss to Schwarzkopf's office, this time on summons to explain a shortage of artillery soldiers due to restructuring.

As soon as they walked in, Schwarzkopf said: "I know who's talking, because he's not," referring to McWilliams's boss.

McWilliams was ready. "He had a crystal bowl of peanut M&Ms on his desk," she remembers. "I leaned over and took a handful of them, and put them in military formation.

"'Sir, the Army's like a bag of M&Ms,' I told him. 'There are only so many in a pack.'" Then she explained the challenge in a few sentences.

Schwarzkopf dismissed them, and McWilliams turned to follow her boss out of the office. They hadn't quite reached the door when Schwarzkopf growled, "Major, keep your fucking hands off my M&Ms."

Schwarzkopf's gruff humor gave a nod to the respect McWilliams had garnered with her careful response, a calculated play based on how he wanted to receive information. Walking away from the office after the second successful briefing, her boss looked at her and asked, "How do you do that?"

"I survey the battlefield," she quipped.

McWilliams knew to listen actively, and picked up on what Schwarzkopf had communicated in his inimitable way, throwing pencils and teasing, about how he wanted to receive information. She had been observant enough to notice, perceptive enough to read between the lines, and smart enough to do her homework, and that allowed her to do what her boss could not—communicate effectively with their senior commander.

Reflecting on the experience, McWilliams explains that, "One of the things I learned from observation is that the big boys didn't want a lot of words," she says. "They wanted it simply put." If she hadn't listened and observed, she wouldn't have understood.

McWilliams listened for what Schwarzkopf needed, made sure she delivered it, and earned his respect. What worked with a tough Army general can work in any situation. By observing and listening first, you will know better how to maneuver.

Listening Isn't as Easy as It Seems

The reason that the true attentiveness required for active listening is difficult is because it runs contrary to the functioning of our brains, which are constantly involved in processing inputs in an attempt to predict the future. From a neurological perspective, it is really hard to be in the present, which is where listening happens.

In a 2007 paper, Harvard Medical School neuroscientists Kestutis Kveraga, Avniel S. Ghuman, and Moshe Bar explained the neurological process this way:

> Rather than waiting to be activated by sensations, [the human brain] is constantly generating predictions that help

interpret the sensory environment in the most efficient manner . . . the brain uses all of the statistical regularity in our environment to shortcut processing in similar future situations. The primary principle is that the brain extracts coarse, gist information rapidly, and uses it to generate predictions that help interpret that input. [It] continuously employs memory of past experiences to interpret sensory information and predict the immediately relevant future.[1]

In most of your waking moments, your brain is continuously and rapidly modeling the world as a dynamic system, doing so based on past knowledge and understanding. This has distinct advantages, as many environments, especially the military, require and reward quick study and a bias for action. Leaning too heavily on this capability, however, makes it difficult to truly be able to listen.

The brain's ability to take in information and use it to predict the future is so robust that, using advanced brain-imaging techniques, researchers at Washington University in St. Louis found the processes of recalling the past and imagining the future to be remarkably similar. Specifically, researchers showed the connection between the rapid assessment of facts and just how quickly the human brain uses those facts to model what is to come.[2] The ability to rapidly model the future likely helped our species survive by helping us, for instance, remember which berries had made someone else in the tribe sick and should therefore be avoided. This same rapid modeling is helpful in modern society too, enabling us to assess a situation and make an informed choice with the greatest odds of success. But in the case of a conversation, this cognitive predilection means that we are typically more focused on rapidly forming a response, even in the middle of an exchange, than we are on hearing what our conversation partner is conveying. This neurological truth, exacerbated by formal and informal power structures, explains, for instance, why doctors have been found to interrupt their patients after only eighteen seconds (some estimates are even less).[3]

Cultivating your ability to listen as a leader requires an awareness of this tendency to analyze and predict. This is a crucial first step, because you can't change a habit without an awareness of your own tendencies. Only after making an active effort to combat your default can you suspend this neurological tendency to jump to judgment and instead permit your brain to take in information without seeking to form a prediction of what will come next.

For those of us in military and corporate settings, the bias toward action, a bias that is so helpful in a crisis, interferes with our active listening abilities in more-mundane moments, which in turn limits our ability to take more global perspectives that are so important to the highest functioning environments. Not listening precludes this wider perspective, and in a vicious cycle, the lack of a broader view makes it more challenging to remember simply to listen.

It is not only our subconscious inclinations but also our difficulty in overcoming implicit biases that make listening difficult for many leaders. According to neuroscientist Andrew Newberg, the director of research at the Marcus Institute of Integrative Health in Villanova, Pennsylvania, "We are essentially trapped within our brains looking out at the world and trying to make some sense of it."

The intersectionality of being in the minority—whether you are the only female on a male team or the only person of color in the room—adds a layer of complexity to the ability to listen, because of the concern that not speaking up might belie weakness and diminish authority. This was certainly my experience.

Listening is how we let in other perspectives so that we can broaden our own understandings. It enables us to lead for the good of all, not just for the good of our own egos. It also ensures that we don't miss important information that could be personal but might also include tactical data—operations or logistics, for instance—that requires careful unearthing.

The good news is that the act of effective listening can be broken down into three distinct steps, which I'll outline below. Master these, and you'll expand your skills, your ability to lead others, and your grit. Why grit? Because by listening, you can work smarter, not harder, with a wider perspective and deeper understanding and stronger relationships. This increases your effectiveness and resilience.

Three Steps to Listening Like a Leader: Ask. Listen. Pause.

If you've been a high-performing leader, or aspire to be one, you're probably in good company in your tendency to jump ahead toward a solution. Thoughtfully considering and paying attention to these three components of effective listening will help mitigate those natural tendencies and allow you to better connect to and understand any challenge.

Ask

As one of the first women to fly the Cobra attack helicopter in the Marine Corps, Jeannette Haynie had been working for years to prove herself in an all-male environment, and she guarded her hard-earned respect with a fierce determination.

Even though she was a graduate of the Naval Academy, Haynie knew that joining the Marines and training to fly the Cobra would be tough.

"They say that Cobra pilots eat their young," she says. But she wasn't afraid. In fact, she recalls that "I wanted to do it because it was the toughest community."

Haynie had already endured the challenges of training, which further developed her innate grit. Despite this success, when she was moved from an operational role to a maintenance role, she was rattled by the requirements of the new position.

"I had a confidence issue, especially knowing I was being judged by my gender as well as my performance," she admits when I ask her about the difficulties of the transition. "I thought asking questions would be a sign of weakness."

Facing ongoing challenges in perception as one of the only women in her unit, Haynie was reluctant to seek answers—worried that asking would only demonstrate what she didn't know, worried that she'd consequently lose the respect she had worked so hard to gain.

Looking back, Haynie regrets that it took her as long as it did to start listening and asking questions. With time and experience, her confidence grew. She began to understand that active listening and careful questioning were worth the risk. Her first piece of advice to new and seasoned leaders alike follows from what she learned in her evolution to a more senior leader.

"Number one: Don't be afraid to ask questions or look stupid," Haynie says. "And number two: Ask the damn questions."

It isn't only young leaders who find listening challenging. Major General Dawn Dunlop, whom we met in chapter 3, an Air Force test pilot who also served as commander of the NATO Airborne Warning and Control System (AWACS) force, had to work at "being uncomfortable and asking questions."

Dunlop is as thoughtful and self-assured as any leader I've interviewed. Yet when we delve into the details of how she deployed both grit and leadership skills during her decades of service, she remembers how difficult it was to cultivate the communication skills she would need, and especially the vulnerability required for her to learn what a new position demanded. Dunlop recalls taking a new position as a squadron commander, a position of ultimate responsibility for a large group of aircraft and the pilots and maintenance technicians who fly and service them. She had been working in operations previously, a place where she contributed individually but did not have command authority. As squadron commander, her responsibilities were much more broad. Dunlop initially found herself continuing to focus on the areas where she was most comfortable. She was accustomed to physical stress—test pilots constantly push their own limits and those of their aircraft. Dunlop wasn't used to not knowing things that were central to her role, and as a commander, she felt it was critical to be seen as in control.

"I needed to focus less on the ops and flying piece and more on the command responsibilities," she remembers. "Learning about the pieces that were new to me and how I could best support all our airmen was critical, and put me outside of my comfort zone." Dunlop had worked hard to be competent, to be seen as competent, and it was not easy to move outside what she had done before and admit that she had much to learn.

How did she acclimate to her new command responsibilities? By spending time in each of the sections where she had little or no previous experience. She asked questions, and she listened. Dunlop confesses that it was difficult to allow herself to be vulnerable enough to admit she needed help.

Over time, however, she learned something that all great leaders come to know: there is power in asking questions. It takes confidence to own up to lacking knowledge, and this learned skill comes in part, it seems, from the confidence these leaders acquired through hard experience. Experience teaches that your colleagues will view your asking questions in order to understand as far wiser and more preferable than your pretending that you already know all the answers (especially when you manifestly do not).

Anyone transitioning into a new position or field has much to learn. Asking the questions—alongside doing the work on your own—opens the door to learning critical information, and it also puts you in touch with the people with whom you'll be working. Asking questions and listening demonstrates respect, and in doing so, builds your team.

Asking questions also helps you fulfill that piece of your core purpose that every leader shares: taking care of your people. You can only take care of your people when you know who they are and what drives them. You don't know this until you take time to truly listen.

Brigadier General Rebecca Halstead, West Point's first female graduate to be promoted to general officer, acknowledges the challenge new leaders have coming into an organization for the first time. In the military, when new lieutenants come in to lead their platoons, many of the people under their commands have more experience in the setting than they do. Some have already seen combat, and they all know the ropes of that particular unit. The lieutenant is new on the scene. The same holds true in the corporate world: any leader who is new to the organization is at a disadvantage in terms of information and experience.

Halstead suggests that if she were to do it all over again, "I would sit with my platoon and ask them to tell me their stories. I would ask: Where did you deploy? What did you do? What did you learn? Asking people to share their stories—and then of course listening to their responses!—shows you are invested in your people and willing to learn from them, despite your rank."

Listen

The Chinese symbol for listening, or *ting*, shows just how complex listening truly is. The symbol represents the mind, which includes undivided attention (focus); the ears; the eyes; and the heart. Listening calls on your whole being: body, mind, and spirit.

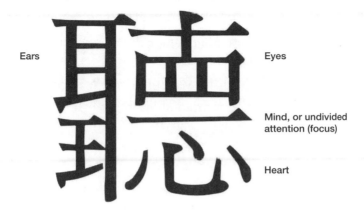

Ears

Eyes

Mind, or undivided attention (focus)

Heart

As both ancient and modern understanding indicates, even across cultures, active listening has as much to do with the posture of the listener as with the specific commitment to listen. It requires both mental and physical engagement, including an attunement to nonverbal cues, your own as well as those of your conversation partner.

Business schools and the military are both recognizing just how important this skill is to master. In the Army's Master Resilience course, research by Shelly Gable at the University of California, Santa Barbara, informs what is known as "the active constructive response,"[4] a listening method that comprises validating (acknowledging what the other person has said) and asking questions, all while considering the physical aspects of listening—aspects that, according to *Army Field Manual 22-101, Leadership Counseling*, include eye contact, an approachable posture, head nods (affirmation), and facial expressions.

In my experience as a young lieutenant, it took many failures before I came to appreciate how important listening was to my role. When I took command of A Company, 1st Aviation Battalion, 2nd Infantry Division, in Korea, I was determined to do better. I was the first woman to lead an Apache line company in the 2nd Infantry Division, and none of my pilots or soldiers had ever worked for a woman. I knew that some were resistant to my presence and others were not comfortable speaking directly to me about their concerns.

Knowing this, I set up a listening session every couple of months where pilots of like rank could come together and talk about anything they wanted, any problems or concerns, without me present. I wanted to open the lines of communication. One of the warrant-officer pilots acted as facilitator and would let me know what came out of the meetings. Nothing contentious or material ever came from those sessions, but the process showed my pilots that I was listening. They knew that I respected their experience and that I cared what they thought. To get to that place of trust, I had to prove that I was open to their ideas. I had to listen first.

Tom Peters, after decades working in the leadership field, published *The Excellence Dividend* as a compilation of the most important lessons he'd learned over the years. Among them? Listening. Peters even gives listening its own chapter: "Listening, the Bedrock of Leadership Excellence."

In that chapter he writes, "I have come to the conclusion . . . that the single most significant strategic strength that an organization can have is not a good strategic plan but a commitment to strategic listening on the part of every member of the organization . . . you can teach listening. You can get better at listening . . . it is a profession that has to be learned."[5]

The four most important words in an organization according to Peters? "What do you think?"

Peters suggests there are two critical pieces to the complex process of "simple listening." The first is respect, and the second is variety. Respect might seem to be self-explanatory, but Peters reminds us that if you ask the four most important words and don't respect the person to whom you are listening, your efforts won't matter. The second aspect, variety, encourages leaders not to listen only to a single group of constituents but to cast their awareness—and their listening—more broadly.

When I think back over my years in uniform and my years in the corporate world as well, Peters's takeaway rings true. My A Company listening sessions were effective only because my pilots knew I trusted them. But I couldn't listen only to the pilots—I had to listen to my crew chiefs, too. And I had to understand the battalion priorities from my commander and the other senior officers. Listening is a 360-degree endeavor. This doesn't mean that you take everything you hear at face value, or that you agree to act on anything without question. Sometimes messaging indicates something in the culture requiring your awareness, and it might even signal a needed change. Always, though, what you hear can inform action and direction. Frankly, when I consider the times that I fail today, in my work, as a volunteer on boards, or even as a parent, it's often because of a failure to listen, or a failure to let people know that I'm listening. Listening, like any skill, takes consistent awareness and practice.

Pause

If listening itself is difficult as we work against our brains' natural tendencies to leap ahead to planning our reaction, one of the most powerful steps in the listening process may be the most challenging: the pause. Creating a moment of time between when your conversation partner stops talking and you respond gives you an important opportunity to internalize what you've heard and to consider its implications and possibilities. It also allows you to reconnect to your own story, purpose, and values, and to those of your organization or mission.

Pausing is difficult for anyone, but especially for a leader programmed to respond rapidly and solve problems proactively. But no meaningful listening can happen without it. When Professor

Julie Lang at the Tuck School at Dartmouth practices the pause with her students, she asks them to listen for ninety seconds, and then to wait fifteen seconds before responding. The pause feels awkward, especially because it is an artificially imposed time, she says. But the exercise teaches leaders to become comfortable with delaying and considering their response. It allows them to internalize all that they've heard. It gives them the time it takes to truly receive the message that has just been communicated.

Brigadier General Rebecca Halstead agrees.

"One of my favorite rules is the three-second rule I learned from the book of the same name," she says. "The thesis of the book is that if we each took three seconds (to listen, discern, pause, settle) before we spoke, we would be a lot happier with what we said! It has been a powerful, effective tool for me as a leader."

The pause alone is not enough, however. In the midst of the pause, a leader has to work not to judge or evaluate, and—this may be the hardest part—not to impose solutions. Instead, a leader learns to truly engage by asking additional questions and paraphrasing. One of the best things you can say after a pause is, "Is there anything else?" or, "Tell me more."

There are times when the most effective pause may be even longer than a squirm-inducing fifteen seconds, particularly when emotions are running hot. In her book *Dare to Lead*, Brené Brown suggests that at times an extended pause is needed in order for listening to be most effective. Facing difficult feedback from her own team, Brown asked for more information, and then promised to think about what she'd heard and come back to them the next day.

In *Dare to Lead*, Brown shares that, "In my research and my life, I've found absolutely no benefit to pushing through a hard conversation unless there's an urgent, time-sensitive issue at hand. I've never regretted taking a short break or circling back after hours of thinking time."[6]

If you need another number to focus on for a pause, try twenty-four. The author Anthony Tjan, whom I referenced in chapter 3, suggests the rule of "24 × 3" as a way to develop optimism, especially in the face of a mentee's ideas that you might be tempted to shoot down:

> The next time you hear an idea for the first time, or meet someone new, try to wait 24 seconds before saying *or thinking* something negative . . . As you gain the ability to listen and pause for a brief 24 seconds before letting the critic in you bubble to the verbal surface, move to the next level and try to do it for 24 *minutes*. At 24 minutes, you are able to give more considered thought to the idea and think more carefully of the many reasons why it might actually work, why it might be better than what is out there, and why it might just topple conventional wisdom.
>
> And yes, you should also work towards the ability to wait 24 hours—one single day—before pondering or verbalizing the cons against something.[7]

Tjan's idea is a synthesis of listening and mindset. To train a mindset, we have to interrupt our natural tendencies to problem solve and act, which is particularly difficult for those leaders who have found reward and success in exactly these two areas. This is an area I may never master. I hope you'll take to it more naturally.

Muddy-Boots Leadership

After taking leadership of my first platoon, and after my book-report debacle, I started (with no small measure of humility) to work on my listening. As excited as I was to be working on aviation knowledge and skills, I had to get out and spend time with the people who worked for me and with whom I worked. I had to get down on the hangar floor.

The crew chief office sat downstairs of the company head-quarters. Unlike the company office, the maintenance office was greasy and dirty. The platoon sergeant's desk might be piled with logbooks as well as aviation parts and oily rags, left in the process of moving from one urgent task to the next. My platoon sergeant was the best noncommissioned officer a lieutenant could hope to have, but I knew that in general, the crew chiefs weren't sure what to do with me. I wasn't sure what to do with them, either. They were mostly young men, hard-living, Harley-riding, beer-drinking guys who listened to Rage Against the Machine. I was an English major from Duke University. We didn't typi-cally discuss book-club selections or weekend plans. I knew it was my job to know them, to listen to them, to understand what it was that made them tick. Without that work, I couldn't do my job of taking care of them, and they would never know I cared.

I pushed through my discomfort and my concern over how I was perceived. I knew that I was the first woman any of them had ever worked for. Heart pounding, I'd walk into the office, as though I knew exactly what I was doing, and as though I wasn't terrified. I'd pick up a logbook, and ask questions about an air-craft. I'd look up at the phase maintenance board, and ask about a part on order, or about maintenance that had been deferred. I'd walk out onto the hangar floor to see a crew chief working on an aircraft, and ask him to show me what it was he was doing.

Little by little I got to know my crew chiefs, and little by little I learned to love them. They were to a person hard-working soldiers, some coming from difficult family situations, all of whom had hopes and dreams and desires. One soldier might never want recognition, but just a little extra time off to go fish-ing. Another might live for the spotlight. I had to make the time and find the space to listen to and understand what mattered to them, and how they could be motivated to do their best work. I had to learn to listen in order to know how to take care of them when they needed it most.

There's a saying in the Army that soldiers don't trust someone whose boots are too shiny, because that shows the person hasn't been out doing the real work with the troops. Leaders have to make themselves available, but even more, leaders have to get out and spend time with the people who are doing the work, in the places they are doing the work. In other words, you need to go out and get your boots muddy. Leaders meet their people where they are. This necessity competes with other urgent matters— the meetings and conference calls and business trips. Listening is hard for leaders in part because it's hard to find the time. The reality is that listening leaders know they won't find time; instead, they will have to make it.

Forcing myself to get out of my flight maps and operations manual and onto the hangar floor and the flight line made me better informed and educated about what my people were doing. It taught me about aircraft maintenance. All of this was important. But most critically, muddy-boots leadership helped me get to know my crew chiefs. I had to get to know my soldiers in order to know what mattered to them. I had to scuff my boots to learn my field, and to take care of my people.

The Army certainly isn't the only organization to recognize the importance of muddy-boots leadership. In his 1982 book, *In Search of Excellence*, Tom Peters termed a related practice at Hewlett-Packard "Management by Walking Around," which we'll shorten to MBWA. MBWA resembles the practice that Toyota calls a "gemba walk," where managers walk to the place where work is being done, observe the work, and talk to employees, with the understanding that seeing problems in context aids problem resolution. The Brits add a slight commonwealth twist to the concept by calling it "Management by Walking About," and Rosabeth Kanter, a professor at Harvard Business School, puts a modern spin on the idea, acknowledging the increase in business travel by calling it "Management by Flying Around."[8] Peters initially borrowed the concept from Ulysses S. Grant, who called it "Commanding by Visiting About," as he rode around on horseback to visit soldiers without the accompaniment of aides. No matter what you call it, it's clear that the idea is important, and its prevalence in the research shows it to be a difficult task to integrate and master.

There is an art to MBWA, however. Without a focus on getting to know your people, MBWA can actually be detrimental. Researchers Anita Tucker and Sara Singer, who studied the use of MBWA in hospitals, were surprised to find a negative impact when the visits by management were focused only on solving problems. Their study indicates the pitfalls of MBWA without a people focus—if MBWA is instituted as a supervisory activity with potentially punitive action, it can have negative consequences. The researchers hint at this understanding with reference to other research in their discussion:

"There may be negative repercussions if senior managers attempt but fail to engage meaningfully with frontline staff. We suspect that the negative consequences arose from soliciting, but not sufficiently addressing, frontline staff's concerns . . . there is a hidden, psychological cost of asking employees for ideas that are subsequently disregarded."[9]

There is a cost to *not* asking the question, but how a leader responds to feedback is just as important.

When I was a lieutenant, our battalion deployed for a month-long training exercise to Fort Hood, Texas. The deployment came at a time when our resources and flight time were significantly curtailed by the federal budget, so our commander jumped at the opportunity. We flew our battalion's twenty-four Apaches cross-country to arrive one blazing-hot Texas day, and over the next month we spent half of our time in the field of the Texas deserts. It was so hot that one night we didn't even set up tents, but slept on cots underneath the camouflage netting.

Our battalion commander was always one to spend time with the pilots and the soldiers. He wanted to be in the action, part of the operation, and that's what made him good at what he did. The regimental commander decided that he would come along on the exercise, too. It was likely a great networking opportunity for him, because he was certainly not interested in being with soldiers or being in the field. The single time he visited us in the woods of Fort Hood is a day I'll never forget.

Because of the heat index during the summer, Fort Hood regulations allowed soldiers in the field to strip off their battle dress uniform (BDU) top, and work in a T-shirt, BDU pants, and boots. That day, like every other I remember there, brought temperatures well into triple digits, with a heat index soaring even higher. The intensity of the sun bleached the blue out of the sky. The commanders in the field saw the uniform allowance as sensible, and as we worked on equipment and prepared briefings and maintained aircraft, the soldiers and pilots were permitted to drop their heavy long-sleeved tops.

In the middle of that brutally hot afternoon, the regimental commander and command sergeant major showed up unannounced. Their shiny black Suburban pulled into the pine-needle-covered assembly area, and both men climbed out in full BDUs with spit-shined boots. I glanced at the suburban, briefly coveting the air conditioning I knew blasted inside, before being overcome with disgust at their arrival. Both senior leaders walked into the tactical operations center and stayed only five minutes. They didn't talk to a single soldier working in the heat, or stay long enough for the heat to dissipate the air conditioning clinging to their starched uniforms. Then they got back into their Suburban and drove away.

As soon as they'd gone, the commanders and noncommissioned officers came out of the headquarters tents and directed everyone to put back on their long-sleeved BDU tops. The regimental commander had come to the field just long enough to reverse the lower-level commanders' decisions, without any attempt to understand what was happening in the field or what the needs and requirements were of the soldiers for whom they were responsible. It is one of the worst examples of leadership I take with me from my years in uniform, though other examples would come up, too. You'll recognize one in a later chapter.

Fortunately for all of us, listening, like grit, is a trainable skill. By developing your ability to truly hear what others have to say, you will be empowered to form connections that facilitate both good leadership and good followership, and you will provide yourself with the information you need to take care of your people and execute on your mission. Whenever you are in doubt about your next course of action, remember the three-step listening process: ask questions, listen, and pause. Make sure you spend time getting your boots muddy, too, interacting with the people who are implementing your organization's mission as well as receiving it. These simple yet deceptively challenging practices are key to your—and your organization's—short-term and long-term success.

EXERCISE

Assess and Plan for Listening

1. Think back to a recent difficult conversation. Did you really, deeply listen? How could you have listened with more attention and less judgment?

2. Practice active listening with a colleague and discuss the objectives before you begin. Force yourself to listen for at least ninety seconds before interjecting. Practice taking a thirty-second pause.

3. Look at your calendar. Have you prioritized one on ones with all of your direct reports? Do you ensure you have clear and consistent communication with your boss? Make certain your schedule allows ample opportunity to ask, listen, and pause.

4. Make a list of key stakeholders in your work. Do you know what motivates each of them? What is important to each of them personally and professionally? If you don't know, sit down and talk with them. Listen. Find out.

5. Do you make sure to get out and spend time with the people who work for you where they are doing their hardest work? Is there a way to connect with them and help solve simple problems for them while you visit? In my work, I had to get out of the office and walk onto the hangar floor. What is the equivalent for your work?

− 5 −

Build Your Resilience

"A good half of the art of living is resilience."

—Alain de Botton

On February 27, 1991, Major Rhonda Cornum was in the back of a Black Hawk helicopter flying fast and low across the Iraqi desert, so low that they would have collided with an American convoy of trucks crawling across the landscape below if the pilot hadn't pulled up in time. The helicopter's crew of eight was responding to the call that an F-16 had been shot down, and the pilot had a broken leg. Cornum, a flight surgeon for the 229th Attack Aviation Regiment, was on board to administer medical aid to the downed pilot.[1]

Just forty-five seconds after they'd passed over the American convoy, green tracers streaked up from the ground "as if we were a lawn mower that had run over a beehive, and the bees were coming up to sting," as Cornum wrote in her memoir, *She Went to War*.[2] The soldiers on the door guns returned fire. One of the shell casings from the machine gun hit Cornum in the face as she lay on the floor, waiting for one stray round to rip through the floor from below.

Then something big hit the helicopter. The aircraft rocked. The engine strained.

Cornum heard the pilot yell, "We're going in!" She grabbed on to the aircraft. She wondered if it was the end. The helicopter crashed at 140 knots onto the desert floor. Everything went dark.

Cornum remembers it was daytime when they crashed, and when she came to it was night. She pushed her way through the wreckage to find her way out of the mangled fuselage. The pain was almost unbearable. Cornum reassured herself by thinking, "Nobody's ever died from pain."

With a PhD in biochemistry from Cornell University, Cornum had been recruited into the Army to work in a research facility in San Francisco. She never expected to deploy.

"I was the least likely person to see combat," she says. "I really joined because I wanted to do research and I didn't want to teach." She ended up liking the Army, particularly the camaraderie and the mission focus.

When Cornum pushed her way out of the wreckage of the Black Hawk, she couldn't stand up or even turn over. When she tried a second time to stand up, she found herself looking up into the barrels of five Iraqi rifles. She noted the soldiers' good uniforms and concluded that they were members of the Republican Guard. Not hearing any other noise, she assumed she was the sole survivor.

One of the soldiers reached down and grabbed Cornum by her right arm. A flash of pain burned through her body. She screamed. The pain told her that her arm was broken, and that his tug had dislocated it as well. Her other arm was also broken. Cornum had been shot, but wouldn't know it until later. The soldier took her by the hair and dragged her behind him.

Cornum, eventually put upright, was forced to walk into a sub-terranean bunker. In a room deep inside the bunker the soldier led her to a circle where one of her crew members was kneeling. Then Cornum and her fellow crew member were taken back outside, pushed into a truck, and taken to a second bunker, and then a third, each time interrogated by a new group of soldiers. Then they were put in another truck, and this time the guard in charge of Cornum sexually assaulted her. She remembers feeling as amazed as she was repulsed. Her hair, matted with blood, covered one eye. Both arms were broken. Her knee was badly injured.

The assault was not the worst part of her captivity. At one bunker Cornum was forced to kneel for a mock execution. She felt the pistol against the back of her head. She waited for the click.

In the midst of this crucible, Cornum understood that how she thought about her situation would define her experience, would determine whether she survived her ordeals or was crushed by them.

The day after Cornum was captured, the war ended. She was repatriated a week later, after eight days in captivity. Cornum used that experience, and her recovery from it, as inspiration to pursue graduate studies in resilience. Now she helps to run the Army's resilience program.

Mindset Is Everything

How you think about difficulties has a great deal to do with how successfully you will navigate them, something that the Army knows well. Many would argue that the greatest weapon in the Army arsenal has nothing to do with helicopters or tanks. The world's greatest warfighters are equipped with psychological training codified in the program toward which Cornum has devoted her energy since returning home from Iraq: the Comprehensive Soldier Fitness program.

Developed in 2009 in response to the devastating effects of post-traumatic stress on soldiers who are required to repeatedly deploy, the training empowers soldiers to build the base of resilience they need to get through sustained challenge. Resilience for purposes of this training is defined as "a set of processes that enables good outcomes in spite of serious threats."[3] Furthering the Comprehensive Soldier Fitness program, the Army worked with the Positive Psychology Center at the University of Pennsylvania to develop the Master Resilience Training course, evidence that many aspects of resilience are teachable.

Master Resilience Training involves developing six core competencies: self-awareness, self-regulation, optimism, mental agility, identifying one's own and others' character strengths, and connection.

The first four chapters of this book—focusing on connecting to your own story, defining your core purpose, developing the right relationships, and cultivating the ability to listen—correlate to three of these six core competencies: self-awareness, understanding your and others' strengths, and connection. In this chapter, we'll target the mental components of grit: optimism, mental agility, and self-regulation.

Training for Optimism

The idea that optimism is a key part of resilience isn't new, but optimism is far from a given. In a study conducted in 1975 by Donald Hiroto and Martin Seligman, the founder of the Positive Psychology Center, the researchers identified something they called "learned helplessness," where animals, and then humans, showed that they will over time accept traumatic treatment with no attempt to change it.[4] In the study, Hiroto and Seligman found that people respond to extreme stressors in a normal distribution, some people falling apart from anxiety and depression and others able to go through what the researchers identified as "post-traumatic growth." This latter group was able to respond resiliently because of an optimistic outlook.

The Penn Resilience Program (of the Positive Psychology Center) defines optimism as "the ability to notice and expect the positive, to focus on what you can control, and to take purposeful action."[5] It relates to, but is separate from, reframing obstacles. It is a manner of encountering circumstance, keeping your attention focused on the positive aspects of the situation and potential outcomes without getting derailed or defeated by the negative ones. While optimism is a way of thinking and a way of being (that is, somewhat innate), it can be learned and honed.

Cornum, whose story opened this chapter, speaks of optimism as a conscious decision to keep your thoughts focused on what you can control, as well as what you're grateful for. While in captivity, Cornum says, "I was grateful I was alive, and I was grateful I was in the war that I was in." Being grateful forces you to look for the things that *are* in your favor, even when it might seem like life itself is conspiring against you. It trains you to focus on what actually is, instead of what hasn't actually happened yet.

Optimism is what helped Cornum bolster herself in those first moments of consciousness after the Black Hawk she was riding in was shot down, when—instead of giving into circumstance—she reminded herself that pain itself wasn't fatal. Cornum summarizes: "Optimistic people believe that a problem is specific and not global." That attitude helped her to take things one day at a time—a moment at a time—in captivity, and to trust that the situation wouldn't last forever. "I felt very confident that I might be there for weeks or even months, but I wasn't going to be there for seven years," she says.

Now that she's had years of teaching the six core components of resilience, she has this to say about the power of mindset:

"One of the most important things you can learn is that what you think, and how you perceive events is totally up to you. You cannot ruminate about the bad part. The enemy may be able to tell you everything else . . . they cannot determine what you think. It is your choice."

Granted, positivity is no panacea. All lessons have their limits. Optimism will get you a long way, but not at the expense of reality. Leadership requires blending optimism with a realistic understanding of circumstances.

This optimism tempered by reality is sometimes referred to as the Stockdale Paradox, named for Admiral James Stockdale. Stockdale was a prisoner of war in Vietnam at the Hanoi Hilton for more than seven years, from 1965 to 1973. Over those years he was tortured more than twenty times. He had no set release date, and no way to know if he would ever see his family again. Still, he persevered and inspired hope while instituting a series of coping methods with the other prisoners. To combat imposed isolation, he developed a tapping code that allowed the prisoners to communicate with each other. Because prisoners are expected not to give any information to their captors past their rank and serial number, an expectation which is not sustainable over prolonged torture, Stockdale put together a schedule over which they could release bits of information. He understood the need to have some small control over a situation. His work with his fellow captives gave them discrete tasks that helped them to get through times that would otherwise be unbearable.

He later went on to earn three stars and became the first Naval aviator to be awarded the Congressional Medal of Honor.

When Admiral Stockdale was asked what caused others to perish while he survived, he responded: "That's easy. Optimism."

This might come as a surprise given Cornum's dogged optimism, but Stockdale understood that optimism has its limits.

In his seminal business-leadership book, *Good to Great*, Jim Collins recounts the comments Admiral Stockdale shared with him:

The optimists "were the ones who said 'We're going to be out by Christmas.' And then Christmas would come and go. Then they'd say, 'We're going to be out by Easter.' And Easter would come, and Easter would go . . . and they died of a broken heart."[6]

Then Stockdale put into words what has come to be called the Stockdale Paradox: "This is a very important lesson. You must never confuse faith that you will prevail in the end—which you never can afford to lose—with the discipline to confront the more brutal facts of your current reality, whatever they may be."

Tempered optimism is key to grit, a crucial ingredient to surviving the most difficult challenges of leadership and of life. Maintaining flexibility in your thinking is a necessary component of this tempered optimism—acknowledging the negative without losing focus on the positive, adopting a new plan when circumstances require.

Building Mental Agility

The next component of the resilience mindset is mental agility, or what the military calls "Battlemind"—a soldier's capacity to face fear and adversity with courage.[7] Cornum's mental flexibility empowered her to adapt her thinking to match her circumstances, and that helped her survive. She admits that prior to being shot out of the Iraqi sky, "I didn't do helpless at all." And yet, as a captive with serious injuries, she was completely dependent on her captors (as well as trusting that her fellow soldiers would come back for her).

"That was probably the most difficult thing, getting someone, especially the enemy, to help you," she says.

Cornum laughs about it now, but the challenge at the time was very real. Without the use of her arms, she could not pull down her flight suit to use the bathroom. When she finally was able to communicate her need to her captors, they seemed flummoxed—

they were not permitted to see an infidel woman without clothing. Finally, one soldier put a robe around her and tied it so that he could assist her with this basic need.

"It's all about plan B," she says. When obstacles arise, "you just have to have a mission change." For Cornum, that meant focusing on keeping herself and her fellow prisoner alive.

How exactly do you cultivate the battlemind, or mental agility? Because mindset is by definition internal, it's a bit of a slippery subject, but one that the Army has worked out a way to teach.

Underlying this module is the work of influential American psychologist Albert Ellis. Ellis developed rational emotive behavior therapy in 1955, which helped make cognitive-behavior approaches central to therapy. His ABC model—short for adversity-belief-consequence—holds that your beliefs about an event drive your emotional and behavioral reactions to said event. Therefore, if you want the freedom to choose how you respond to any particular circumstance—whether it's one you're facing in the moment, or one that happened in your past that is still affecting you—you have to examine and challenge your beliefs.

To train for a more positive response in the moment, the Army's resilience program offers a reframing exercise. The training suggests using "sentence starters" to help reshape thoughts. This practice suggests that a different perspective can come from restating the challenge, provided one avoids the "common pitfalls" of "dismissing the grain of truth, minimizing the situation, rationalizing or excusing one's contribution to a problem, and weak responses."[8]

Some of the sentence starters suggested include:

- *That's not completely true because* . . . This prompt requires you to prove your own assumptions and recognize contradicting evidence.

- *A more optimistic way of seeing this is . . .* This helps you actively seek the positive aspects of whatever issue you're facing.

- *The most likely implication is . . .* This sentence starter nudges you to take a broader perspective. Because the phrase *most likely* is contained within it, it also helps you keep your answers rooted in reality instead of conjecture.

Answering these questions can be performed on your own, either inside your own head or in a journal. I find that writing—and then reading back—my answers to these questions helps me be more objective and reveals insights that I might not have discovered otherwise. Another effective tactic is to answer these questions in conversation with someone who I know supports me, especially if this person is outside my immediate work environment. This brings together mental agility and connecting with others. Grit doesn't operate in a vacuum.

Erin McShane is not only one of the first women to go through the Army's Ranger School but also one of relatively few to graduate from the combat-engineer (sapper) course. McShane remembers the sapper course as being the hardest.

"On the day of Boat PT [physical training], we woke up long before the sun and assembled next to our Zodiac boats, inflatable black boats weighing over three hundred pounds each. Though we only had a mile to carry them and six soldiers to a boat, the instructors made sure that every inch of that mile was painful. They stood on top of the boats, yelling for us to pick up and put them down, overhead press the boat, and do a number of terrible exercises . . . I never want to do it again."[9]

"I have a personal rule: never complain," she writes in *Shave Your Head*, the guide she put together for other women considering Ranger School. "Things could always be worse and you always have a better lot than someone else."

I ask her if, for all of her successes, she can recall a failure, and how she came to work through it.

McShane remembers a patrol in Ranger School. Patrols are used to evaluate soldiers in different leadership roles, and Mc-Shane had already served as patrol leader. She wanted to help her fellow Ranger candidates, and mentioned an idea to her colleague filling the patrol-leader position. The Ranger Instructor pulled her aside and gave her feedback: she shouldn't be interfering in her fellow soldier's decision making. She needed to stay back and support. She was downgraded for her role in the patrol.

She was frustrated. She had thought she was helping, but she was getting in the way.

Later, a mentor helped her think differently about that failure.

"I learned that my failure was in what I did, and not in who I was," she says. "Failure is a result of the methods chosen, and not of the person. It was such an important thing to take away."

It is wisdom I would have liked to have had. Despite having lived through challenges in uniform, I found myself doubting my capabilities in the new arena of the corporate world. In the middle of my first year at business school, I jumped into the fray of interviews for summer internships with an initial focus on consulting. After the on-campus interviews, a particular consulting firm invited me to come in for a subsequent and final round of interviews in Boston. This firm was known for the academic prowess of its consultants, many of whom spoke multiple languages and held more than one PhD. While I'd done well in the early interview rounds, once it came to packing my bags to head to Boston for the final rounds, I started to doubt myself.

I called my dad from my apartment in a hundred-year-old farmhouse in Lebanon, New Hampshire. My travel bag was spread out on my bed, half-packed. I paced back and forth. My dad had always been my anchor (a crucial role on my dream team, as I discussed in chapter 3). I told him how nervous I was about my interview, and how utterly ridiculous it was that they'd even asked me to come talk to them.

His response showed me how to reframe the damaging monologue playing in my head.

"Your experiences are just as incomprehensible to them," he said. "You've been through bigger challenges. Besides, they asked you to come, and they wouldn't waste their own time." He ended with one of his typical aphorisms, saying, "Remember that every single person gets out of bed in the morning and puts on their pants the same way, one leg after the other."

I hung up the phone. The afternoon light filtered in through the window. Outside, spring buds pushed their way out on tree branches. I thought about it—literally visualized people in their respective bedrooms pulling on pants, one leg at a time. I remembered flying, the total mastery and the confidence it required. It was a conscious effort to smooth out my wrinkled thoughts, taking my scattered fears and organizing them neatly. I had overcome more-difficult things than an interview, no matter where it was, and had done them well. I closed up my travel bag, and focused on the work I'd done to prepare. I didn't get an offer, but I'd given it my best.

It isn't only our interior monologues that sabotage us, though. Without care, we can easily be brought down by negativity in others, whatever their motivation. As Cornum notes, "You need to have enough self-efficacy to not be negatively influenced by what people expect of you. You will be surrounded by people with low expectations . . . mediocrity really loves company."

It's far too easy for many of us to succumb to the negativity, the doubts, the worst-case thinking, and the false narratives that come out of others' mouths, whether they are well-meaning or not. Redirecting your thoughts requires the earlier work of understanding your story and staying focused on your core purpose, and it requires the continual work of remaining positive, disregarding negativity, and continuing forward against the odds. As Theodore Roosevelt reminded us: It is not the critics that count. And once in the arena, we all have to do the work to stay focused. That work requires self-regulation.

Fostering the Ability to Self-Regulate

The third of the core competencies of resilience that relate to mindset is self-regulation, which the Army's Master Resilience Training workbook defines as the ability to "regulate impulses, emotions, physiology, and behaviors to achieve goals, express emotions appropriately, and stop counterproductive thinking."[10] Imagining a realistic worst-case scenario helps you self-regulate by practicing calm even in the face of failure, and thinking through your response *before* you're in the moment. Some circumstances require a more immediate approach.

While reframing and thinking through your response to failure (as we covered in the section on building mental agility earlier in this chapter) are important, both take time for reflection and consideration. Real life doesn't always offer the time and space to support this kind of work. There are times that require a more immediate approach. Mission focus, especially in the cockpit, requires 100 percent concentration. A few pilot tricks can help make this exercise work: flight planning, checklists, and rituals.

The first, flight planning, involves preparing for what has to be done. This preparation would include taking into account contingencies—related to your own limitations and to challenges inherent in the mission—in order to help you anticipate what might come up. One specific way to think about this is to write down in advance anything that might interfere with focus. Then make a decision to put such things aside. Put them mentally into a box, and decide to address them at a later time.

As a part of flight planning, compartmentalization is a temporary solution to get through a period requiring extreme focus in the face of difficulty. The concept is named for how it might be visualized: consider that you have a compartment, or a box, into which you can put a concern or a distraction. The terms *concern* and *distraction* may seem euphemistic at best for a serious challenge, but temporarily consider that such things might be packaged up or put away. Visualize putting them into a box and then closing and securing that box. After the mission, after the flight, you can take them back out again, but before you take off, they have to be put away.

This technique does not suggest that you try to ignore a real problem, or in any way disregard its implications or its impact. Instead, compartmentalization recognizes that focus on the work at hand may require special measures. This compartmentalization takes work, and is another learned skill—one I did not learn successfully until after much practice. The best example of my own failure to compartmentalize was during an instrument check ride (a certification test) as a lieutenant newly assigned to Fort Bragg. My check ride was scheduled with a warrant-officer instructor pilot whom I liked and respected, though he was outspoken in his discomfort about flying with (and working with) women. He was never unkind, or unfair, but I remember one conversation in which he bristled at finding out I would sleep in the pilot tent in the field.

"I've been married for ten years, and my wife has never even heard me fart," he told me. I didn't have a response to that, but I felt his discomfort every time we were around each other.

Both of us were on edge before and during the check ride. It was a summer afternoon in North Carolina, and thunderheads towered in an otherwise blue sky. The heat of the day rose from the fields, and I wrestled the air currents that were pushing us higher over the agricultural land and dropping us down in the relatively cooler air over the forests. The combination of discomfort flying together and the challenges of the check ride were too much. For the only time in my years in aviation, I failed to keep my altitude within the 100-foot margin that was required. And for the first and only time in my years in uniform, I failed my check ride.

I was mortified. I felt the weight of the fishbowl—my performance reflected on me and, as I saw it, on all women who might follow. I had confirmed what may have been this instructor's suspicions that I wasn't up to the task, that I didn't belong. None of these were productive thoughts. I would have benefitted from Erin McShane's mentorship—remember that a failure reflects on the technique chosen, not on you.

There was no time for me to indulge my own shame. If I were to wallow in my misery, I would never rectify what had happened. I had to put away my mortification, close it up in a box, and work forward. My commander scheduled me for a follow-up check ride with an instructor pilot in another company. The flight came with the same weather challenges, but none of the anxiety, of the first. I transmuted the significantly higher stakes of the second check ride into sheer determination to succeed. (Had I failed this check ride, I would have been grounded.) Our flight was textbook. I kept altitude in the fluctuating air temperatures and landed with a restored sense of accomplishment. During my first check ride, I failed to compartmentalize anxiety unrelated to the task at hand. During the second ride, given the stakes, I had no choice but to compartmentalize. I had learned to put unrelated concerns temporarily aside.

The second tactic involves using checklists. In Atul Gawande's book *The Checklist Manifesto*, checklists gained the respect all pilots already knew they deserved. Gawande examines examples in aviation and medicine, among other fields, suggesting that in some cases the work has become so technically complex that checklists are necessary to reduce error based on incompetence.

"The volume and complexity of what we know has exceeded our individual ability to deliver its benefits correctly, safely, or reliably," writes Gawande.[11]

The key aspects of preparing a plane for flight are subject to detailed checklists, which pilots are required to follow to reduce the probability of error. No matter how well I knew—or had memorized—the preflight or run-up procedure, I followed the checklist. All pilots did. And while a checklist may seem like over-kill in the office, it can be helpful. There's a reason they're considered a best practice in high-risk operational settings, as they give you guidance, ensure you don't miss anything, and perhaps most important, reduce cognitive load, freeing up mind space for other concerns.

Aviators have protocols for everything *in* flight, too. While not technically checklists, these protocols are specific and detailed, and every bit as important. Our most important in the Apache—where we were seated in tandem, unable to look over at one an-other—was the three-way positive transfer of controls.

"You have the controls," my backseater would say to me, indi-cating that I was in charge of piloting the aircraft.

"I have the controls," I would confirm.

"You have the controls," he would answer.

That three-part communication was required every time.

Another kind of prescribed action helps to focus you on the task at hand and connect you to purpose, both of which are as-pects of self-regulation. That action is ritual. There are two different kinds of rituals that help with self-regulation. The first is the daily ritual, and the second is the ritual of a given experi-ence. Pilots can be superstitious about rituals. When I was flying cross-country with a new backseater once, he shared his own su-perstition: on every flight, he had a pencil in one pocket, always the same pocket, and a pen in the other, also always the same. He spent time justifying his ritual to me, as though expecting I would—and should—adopt it myself.

I'd adopted my own rituals in earlier adventures. After attend-ing the Army's Airborne School following my freshman year of college, I had trained as a skydiver, earning my advanced license after more than a hundred jumps. From my very first jump, I had my ritual for every flight to altitude. A few minutes before the door opened, I'd ask a fellow jumper to check my equipment. This was both a visual and a physical comfort, seeing and feeling a colleague's hands passing over the lanyard to the drogue chute to be sure it wasn't twisted or in any way encumbered, checking the release pin on the reserve. After this check, I closed my eyes, said the Lord's Prayer, and prayed for the people I loved. When the door opened, I was ready to jump.

It turns out that there is plenty of both social science and brain science supporting the importance of rituals. Francesca Gino and Michael Norton, behavioral scientists and professors at Harvard Business School, looked at the use of rituals by everyone from high-performing athletes to those experiencing grief, and found such use associated with greater confidence and reduced anxiety. "In one recent experiment," Gino and Norton write in *Scientific American*,

> people received either a "lucky golf ball" or an ordinary golf ball, and then performed a golf task; in another, people performed a motor dexterity task and were either asked to simply start the game or heard the researcher say "I'll cross fingers for you" before starting the game. The superstitious rituals enhanced people's confidence in their abilities, motivated greater effort—and improved subsequent performance. These findings are consistent with research in sport psychology demonstrating the performance benefits of pre-performance routines, from improving attention and execution to increasing emotional stability and confidence.[12]

Rituals of experience connect you to core purpose, as the military knows well. The commissioning oath is laden with both the weight of words and of tradition, a public ritual involving raising your right hand and pledging to fulfill certain duties and loyalties. The gravity of this public statement, made in a formal way, in a formal environment, cannot help but impress itself on your psyche. Parades, promotion and retirement ceremonies, and other events are also carefully scripted and rehearsed. These rituals connect you repeatedly to your pledge, your adopted purpose. They are comforting in their rootedness in history, in their power and repetition. Rituals serve the need to do something concrete and prescribed in the face of the unknown. Taken together, these techniques support your ability to get through the hardest times with grit.

Staying Focused over the Long Term

Grit can propel you to seek out challenging opportunities and help you get through finite and specific difficult circumstances. But perhaps the toughest challenges are those that require grit and mental resilience over the long haul.

Sara Faulkner made it through the sustained physical and psychological difficulties of the Coast Guard's notorious rescue-swimmer training—a crucible I'll share more about in chapter 6—but it was the career-long struggle in a climate of weak leadership and hostile environments that almost broke her.

"I was sexually harassed in my first unit by the shop supervisor," she says. "I didn't do anything about it. The shop supervisor was a 'cool guy,' and people liked him, but everyone started to get uncomfortable [with his behavior toward me]." While Faulkner tried to take it in stride, "After a year, I filed a complaint."

After she filed her complaint, things got worse.

"The command made my life a living hell," she says. It got so bad that this competitive fighter of a swimmer, who had trained for decades to exceed expectations and stay strong in the face of adversity, almost didn't come into work one day. Finally, she filed charges.

When the assaulter was arrested, the reprisals she endured were worse than the assault.

"My own command tried to get me kicked out of the Coast Guard. I was sent against my will to a Navy hospital to be analyzed at a psych ward, and then to my district admiral who tried to bribe me. He told me if I dropped my complaint, he'd reassign me, but was going to send me to a unit without rescue swimmers."

The scare tactics didn't work.

"I said no. I think he was shocked," Faulkner recalls. She persevered through sustained difficulty by reconnecting to her story and her core purpose. "I was a rescue swimmer. That's where I wanted to work." She went back to her unit.

After a later assignment proved similarly challenging, Faulkner almost left the Coast Guard. "Then another command master chief who came from another aviation specialty talked to me and convinced me to stay," she says.

This master chief said something that helped Faulkner find the perspective that empowered her to keep going. "He told me I was a role model for other women."

Faulkner shares this story a year after her Coast Guard retirement, with a voice that sounds hopeful that her example might encourage others.

"At every single station I have had to fight to be treated equally," Faulkner says, with noticeable emotion.

"I wouldn't want a daughter of mine to go through what I did," she says. "I'd tell anyone who wants it: You go, girl, but watch out."

Faulkner's experiences are, unfortunately, far from unique. Many of the leaders I interviewed for this project suffered assaults and worse. Most experienced what are now referred to as "micro-aggressions," resulting in the exhausting and relentless degradation of a person in an environment not accepting of someone for reasons over which that person has no control. The direct physical assaults have negative short-term and long-term consequences, and the microaggressions do too. This kind of environment con-

sumes enormous amounts of energy and can be a distraction of staggering proportion. Faulkner lived it, and she was not alone.

What I remember about enduring years of microaggressions in the military is how much physical energy it took to stay focused and not be pulled into the morass of negativity. It's easier to be negative than not, and it takes consistent and dedicated commitment to move ahead and not be pulled down. I remember at Fort Bragg going home with a great feeling one day, having flown a successful mission and feeling a momentary hint of the camaraderie I'd craved during most of my years in uniform. That night I relaxed at home alone, which for me often meant making a simple dinner and watching *Law and Order* reruns on TNT.

At 9:00 p.m., two warrant officers called me. They were clearly out drinking, and they wanted to come by my condo. Neither had been there before. In fact, there was no reason for them to know where I lived. They were insistent, and I was as insistent that they were not welcome. But I was shaken. I locked my doors, turned out the lights. It was a reminder, like so many others, that I was not a part of the team, as I'd just that afternoon allowed myself to imagine I was. I'm not sure whether I was more afraid for my physical safety or more broken by the clear indicator of how I was considered—as a target for untoward advances. After the fear came sheer exhaustion. Experiences like this were not isolated, and happened at random. I had to keep my guard up at all times. What did I do about it? I walked up those hangar steps the next day into my office as though nothing had happened, and I focused on the next task ahead.

While this particular kind of microaggression was more a part of my military time, the drain of negativity it produced isn't unique to the military. When I was nineteen and climbing Denali, one team member complained continuously. The physical challenge of climbing Denali was greater than anything I'd ever experienced (or have experienced since), by orders of magnitude. This team member's negativity was toxic and draining.

I remember forcing myself to smile and make positive comments. According to our team journal, written by that same gloomy team member, I was annoying in my overuse of the word *awesome*. I have no doubt that his perspective was true. He did not summit, but turned back due to headaches. I don't know if physically he might have had a chance to make it, but I am certain that his fatalism did nothing to help him (or others) in a pursuit that required every ounce of his being.

Everyone who encounters a hostile work environment inevitably comes to a point where she has to ask herself if it is worth it to continue. Does it make sense to spend so much energy on combating environments where leadership does not support your efforts, or at least does not take steps to counter the forces that are buffeting you, or where team members themselves are toxic? Only you can answer that question in a given situation. If you don't have a resilient mindset, adversity causes only misery. Optimism, mental agility, and self-regulation are what help you transcend, or at least move through, adversity.

One thing I believe as much as any other is that success is possible only with optimism, and that the world needs more realistic optimists. There are a million reasons you can't do something. You have to focus on the reasons you can.

Choosing to focus on the positive, on what you can control, and on taking action comes naturally for some, and through hard-earned experience for others. Leaders know they must consciously cultivate the mindset that helps you move forward, growing as you do. Flight planning, checklists, and rituals will help.

Hunting the Good Stuff

This exercise, taken from the Army's Master Resilience Training, mirrors what you may have heard of as gratitude journaling. It is specifically intended to help you develop a more positive or optimistic mindset, and it is something you can do every day to build the mindset needed for grit.

1. Each day, record in a notebook three good things that happened that day.

2. Then, next to each positive event, write a reflection about one or more of the following topics:

   - Why did this good thing happen?

   - What does this good thing mean to you?

   - What can you do tomorrow to enable more of this good thing?

   - What ways do you or others contribute to this good thing?

Reframing a Problem

Walk yourself through the process of thinking agilely by using some of the sentence starters in the section on building mental agility.

1. Think of a situation that is causing you difficulty or stress.

2. Choose at least two of the three sentence starters, and answer them in your journal.

3. Then ask someone from your dream team to feed you the same sentence starters, and talk out your answers. Notice whether one process revealed more or different insight than the other.

Self-Regulation

The Army's Master Resilience Training says that "Managing energy is essential to optimal performance. Deliberate breathing is a tool used to gain control of your physical state, bring your focus to the present moment, and prepare you to perform more optimally."

To practice deliberate breathing:

- Think of something in your life that causes stress.

- Practice rhythmic breathing, breathing in for the same counts as you breathe out, for five to ten breath cycles.

- After completing those breath cycles, write notes on your thoughts, emotions, and physical reactions. How many counts did you use to breathe in and out? How did you feel? What did you think? How could you bring yourself to a place of greater focus?

Changing Thinking Patterns

To avoid thinking traps and find new approaches to a current stressful situation, think through your answers to each of the following questions:

1. What is the evidence for and against my thoughts?

2. Did I express myself? Did I ask for information?

3. How did others and/or circumstances contribute?

4. How did I contribute?

5. What is changeable? What can I control?

6. What is the specific behavior that explains the situation? What specific area of my life will be affected?

Part Three

LAUNCH

— 6 —

Turn Your Nose to Face the Wind

"Life is either a daring adventure or nothing at all."

—Helen Keller

Do you know which way you take off in an Apache helicopter? When I ask that question to audiences, the answer I hear from leaders around the country at all levels, in all industries, in almost every audience, is "up." That, of course, is the end goal. But when taking off in an attack helicopter, as in every other aircraft, your first step isn't to pull pitch skyward. The first thing you do on takeoff in any aircraft is to point the nose to face the wind.

While a helicopter generates lift from the rotation of the rotor blades, that lift is increased by the wind. When you take off toward the wind, the resistance provided by the air coming toward you generates an upward force on the blades, and the aircraft lifts off the ground.

It's the same with fear—fear is just another form of resistance. The most effective way to navigate fear is by facing toward it. If you use the resistance, it will help you rise.

Any time you take any action, you will face resistance, whether it is internal, like fear or negative thoughts, or external, such as negative reactions from those around you. Flying a helicopter taught me that facing a new assignment, a new challenge, or an obstacle of any kind requires seizing the initiative, taking every opportunity you're given, and searching out the chance to excel. The only way to rise above resistance is to face it head-on and meet it with appropriate power for the force of lift to overcome the force of gravity. You can't let yourself be paralyzed by fear. You can't let yourself be pulled down by those who don't want to go for the ride. As a leader, you have to learn to use fear to help you fly.

Overcome Resistance by Exceeding Expectations

If one thing came out of the interviews for this project, it is that leaders commit not only to facing the wind but to performing exceptionally. To a one, the women I spoke with pushed themselves beyond what was required of them.

The Greeks have a word describing a broader ethos: *arete*, a striving for excellence in every area. This concept of *arete* eschews mediocrity, expecting the best in each area of life and performance. *Arete* must be part of the leader's ethos today, too.

To have the best chance of success in your field, your performance must be stellar—*arete* must be your goal. This is not perfection, but it is true excellence. If you are a leader in a competitive environment, you're already inclined toward this level of high performance. If you're a leader who is underrepresented in your field, you may perceive such exceptional performance as necessary (and you'd be right). This kind of performance may still (and studies show likely will) result in harsh judgment, but your exceptional performance can earn you the seat at the table that would otherwise be lacking.

Pioneering Coast Guard rescue swimmer Sara Faulkner had an innate understanding that she would have to exceed the standards to get through her rigorous training.

Faulkner joined the US Naval Sea Cadet Corps in high school, a leadership-development program that teaches children ages ten and older about Naval disciplines. She was a member of the only all-female division, named for Betsy Ross. It was on a cadet trip on the USS *Kitty Hawk* that Faulkner decided she wanted to swim for the Coast Guard, because the Navy rescue swimmers Faulkner met on board told her that they only sat around on circling helicopters, and that if she wanted to do real rescue-swimmer work, she should join the Coast Guard.

When Faulkner graduated high school, she went after her dreams. She started by joining the Coast Guard. But the Coast Guard wasn't interested in her dreams.

"The Coast Guard said that there were no female rescue swimmers and alluded to the fact that there never would be, explaining that they had broken away from the Navy rescue swimmers twelve years prior and had higher standards," she recalls.

Faulkner was, as she says, "pissed." Right away, her resilience mindset started kicking in. "I immediately envisioned myself as the first woman to make it through."

After waiting nearly five years for a rescue-swimmer training slot to open up, and extending her service in the Coast Guard multiple times just to keep her name on the list, Faulkner was finally given a space. While there was one other female rescue swimmer who had trained in the earlier program run by the Navy, no woman had graduated from the Coast Guard's program.

Before her training began, Faulkner was assigned to work with an existing group of rescue swimmers.

"Half were cool about me being there, and half weren't," she says. "But even the half that were didn't think I would make it through."

She started the training as one of fifteen students. "When you show up," she says, "you look around and wonder who will be there at the end, and you just pray you'll be one of the last ones standing. Nobody knows if they'll make it all the way through."

As soon as the sixteen-week course began, students and instructors alike started talking, trying to undermine Faulkner's confidence. "They'd tell me about the girls who had almost made it but failed," Faulkner says. She asked herself what the most likely outcome of her training would be: "Part of me thought that I could see me failing, but part of me doubted it." It was the doubting part that both kept her hopeful and prompted her to train harder.

"I knew that, as a female, I wasn't as strong as the males going through the training," she continues. "So I made sure I was way, way over what the minimum requirements were to pass the test."

The test required that fifty push-ups be completed in two minutes, so Faulkner trained to be able to perform eighty. It also required applicants to be able to complete five pull-ups and five chin-ups, and Faulkner didn't stop training until she could do sixteen of each.

"I made sure I had that extra room to compensate for a day with the flu, an injury, or the inevitable loss of performance due to the body actually breaking down," she tells me.

The mental component of the test was by far the worst, though. The final segment required candidates to wait in the concrete-block locker room while the instructors took one swimmer at a time to the pool area to gauge their performance during a multiple-survivor scenario. While candidates waited for their turn to be tested, they listened to what sounded like chaos.

"There was a lot of noise—screams and pounding," Faulkner says. "The test is as much psychological as it is physical.

"I never let them know I knew they were screwing with me," she continues. "They definitely tried to get me to quit. But I took whatever they gave me without complaint or showing any emotion. I just did it even though I knew it was completely messed up."

Despite her ability to keep her thoughts focused on her preparation and on not succumbing to the invitations—or outright prodding—to lose her cool, Faulkner says she wasn't sure what the outcome of her test would be. "I never had faith it would all work out," she admits. "I knew rescue swimmers were proud of being the only all-male specialty in the Coast Guard. They could have failed me at any time just because they wanted to. I always had that hanging over my head." In the end, she was one of five (out of the original fifteen) to make it through.

Faulkner also displayed the tempered optimism that the Stockdale Paradox, which we covered in chapter 5, suggests is so crucial for survival. "I would visualize the instructors trying to unjustly fail me, and it would inspire me to train harder."

The strategy paid off: "My numbers declined quite a bit on my final physical test," Faulkner says. "So had I not prepared for that, I could have not made it.

"When I realized they were letting me pass rescue-swimmer school, I was actually shocked it was happening," she continues. When it was all over, "the master chief of the school stopped me in the hallway at school. He said exactly this: 'All the rumors are true. I was never going to let a female become a rescue swimmer. I didn't think they could do it. You changed my mind.'"

Faulkner used her fear as motivation to exceed the standards. It didn't necessarily make her journey any easier, but it brought her rewards on multiple levels—not only the qualification and career that she sought, but also the knowledge that her success had helped to change the perception of women's capacity to perform, and to excel.

Train Early, Train Often

As the military knows, training and preparation are the best antidotes to fear. A focus on continuing education itself is necessary preparation for increased responsibilities as you become more senior. A number of the leaders I interviewed for this book brought up the importance of taking advantage of training opportunities as early and as often as possible, even identifying this focus as a key factor in their success. Ensuring that you prioritize this training and experience early in your career, when you have more time for it, is critical. Several women expressed regret that they had not better prioritized additional training early on, because the increasing demands of both career and personal life make such training harder to pursue over time.

Major General Tracy Garrett—who retired as the highest-ranking woman in the Marine Corps Reserve—offers the following advice to all new leaders, from the perspective of a decades-long career:

"You have a relatively short time to become excellent. That has to be your focus."

Amy McGrath followed that advice. The first woman to fly the F/A-18 in combat in the Marines, McGrath found no substitute for excellence. After qualifying for the front and back seat in the F/A-18, she qualified on carriers (taking off from and landing on an aircraft carrier at sea). Later, McGrath was selected to attend the highly competitive Marine Division Tactics Course (MDTC), the Marine equivalent of Top Gun, for training fighter pilots in air-to-air combat. The selection process for MDTC is fierce: The commanding officers of each squadron select one aviator who must meet strict criteria and who shows the most potential and aptitude to participate in MDTC. To be selected, the aviators need to have been a mission commander, have more than five hundred hours of flight time, be a low-altitude tactics instructor and a fighter-attack instructor. Those who successfully complete the course are identified by a patch worn on their uniform.

"If you walk into a room with an MDTC patch on your left shoulder," McGrath says, "you know that, 'Hey, I've got this on my uniform for a reason. I earned this. This is a challenge, but I can do this.'" But it didn't excuse her from continuing to exceed expectations at every possible turn.

Even after earning her MDTC patch, McGrath continued her relentless pursuit of excellence. "There's never a break," she says. "There's never a time when you can say 'I've graduated, and now I can relax.' There is no substitute for hard work. To perform and do well, you're going to have to work your ass off."

McGrath never stopped pushing, even after she left the military. From the moment she retired, she simply adjusted course: her commitment to growth and challenge has led her to run for the US Senate against Mitch McConnell, an entrenched incumbent in her home state of Kentucky.

Alda Siebrands's story offers another excellent example of what comes from actively seeking challenge and opportunity. When Siebrands left her home on an eighty-acre farm in northern Iowa for college at the University of Iowa in the 1960s, she played basketball on the half court, all that was permitted for women. Most women at that time went on to nursing or teaching, but Siebrands wasn't interested in either. Instead, she signed up for the Peace Corps, and headed to Costa Rica. After two years in the jungle, she knew she wanted more adventure.

"At the time, the Army had a campaign to 'See the world,'" Siebrands says. The only way a woman could earn a commission in the Army then was OCS or a direct commission requiring an application with a college degree. Siebrands applied and was accepted into the Army. This was just the beginning of her adventures.

"I reported to Fort McClellan, Alabama, where they trained the women officers," she says. "There were four platoons, about two hundred women. I chose Signal Corps, because it seemed like it had better opportunities for field time," she says.

Soon after she began work, she had a chance to go to jump school (Army Airborne School). She took it, and reported to her first duty station—Fort Bragg—with jump wings on her chest.

It's worth commenting that in the 1970s, there were few women anywhere in the military. Airborne School is challenging training for Army leaders. Jumping would have been the last thing on most people's minds, especially on that of a woman entering the military at a time when women in the military were almost unheard of. For Siebrands, it was just the beginning.

"I checked in to the 50th Signal Battalion in 1977, which was a great opportunity to keep jumping," she says. "They produced their own jumpmasters too, and my boss asked me if I wanted to go to the training. I said sure, though I didn't think I'd make it through, and asked him if I washed out if I could have another chance. He said yes."

The all-male Army Special Forces taught the Jumpmaster School then, which boasted a withering 50 percent attrition rate. Siebrands was up for the challenge. She succeeded her first time through as a distinguished graduate, the first woman ever to complete the course.

"When you show you can do it, the gender differences just disappear most times," she says.

Siebrands recommends that leaders "see what the opportunities are and be ready for them. I never turned down any course that came available, and each of those opportunities opened up new paths."

She would continue to look for opportunities for challenge. When Siebrands heard about flight school, which had only recently opened to women, she started looking for a way to go. After fifteen months at Fort Bragg, she went to Fort Rucker to begin helicopter flight training, starting out in the TH-55 and then transitioning to the UH-1. She graduated in 1979.

"I requested Korea, because post-Vietnam stateside assignments didn't have much flying," she says. Though her battalion commander tried to slot her into the safest assignment, flying VIP missions, Siebrands wouldn't have it.

"When I was there I transitioned to the OH-58. We got to fly all over the country. There were a lot of single-pilot opportunities, and I had to get DMZ qualified."

McGrath and Siebrands took advantage of every chance for training, development, and contribution that came their way—the more challenging, the better. Each challenge they surmounted helped the women get more comfortable with stepping up to the next level, even when that next level was filled with unknowns.

Take Risks

Facing the wind by taking risks and seizing opportunities is a powerful way to give yourself and your career more lift. Two separate studies of women general officers emphasize the importance of visibility for leadership progression, with that visibility coming from expertise that is gained through experience in challenging roles. The 2013 report of the Director's Advisory Group on Women in Leadership in the CIA recommends that as their careers progress, women "should muster the courage and seize opportunities to accept highly visible jobs when opportunities arise."[1] Similarly, Marianne S. Waldrop's dissertation on women generals indicates that leaders "embraced the philosophy of taking the hard, aggressive leadership positions to be competitive with their male counterparts . . . Success on promotion boards resulted from participants taking high-risk positions of command or operational staff positions."[2]

Siebrands is a great example of a leader with a willingness to take risks. After leaving the Army, she transitioned to the Coast Guard, where her audacity and her willingness to jump (quite literally) became the stuff of legend. She is known especially for an unusual rescue mission off the coast of Washington state.

It's worth telling the next story from two perspectives. Before I made contact with Siebrands, our mutual acquaintance, Hank Cramer, himself a retired Special Forces colonel, sent me an email:

> One day in the mid-1990s, I was working as the State 911 Manager and had dropped into the Port Angeles/Clallam County 911 Center. I asked the manager, Naomi Wu, if anything interesting was going on, and she said "Yes!" She explained that a call had come in that a fishing boat had sunk in the Strait of Juan de Fuca, leaving an elderly man to swim for it. The rescue helicopter was out of range, over on the coast near Forks. BUT . . . there was a USCG helicopter in the air locally. It had no rescue swimmer, it was an instructor pilot taking a rookie for a check-ride in the H-65. They found the old man and lowered the cable to him, but he was too hypothermic to be able to grab the cable and put on the harness. "So what happened?" I asked. Naomi tells me, "The instructor pilot turned the controls over to the co-pilot, then SHE jumps out of the helicopter into the water to get the guy!" I said, "Damn, that's got to be Alda Siebrands." She asked "Who?" So I explained that I only knew one female pilot in the USCG, and only one decisive and unconventional enough to dive into the ocean from the aircraft in which she was the command pilot. I was right, it was Alda.

When I talk to Siebrands, she doesn't change much of Hank's story.

"It was another nice day," she says. "We were out for a routine flight in the San Juans with extra operations folks on board orienting them to the area. There was a fourteen-foot fishing boat off Pillar Point that had waited too long when the weather came in. Three men were on board, an older man and his son and another man in his forties. The boat flipped over in the breakers. The third man swam for shore, and though we never recommend leaving the boat, he ended up making it and crawled onto shore just as a couple was walking down to the beach. They called the Coast Guard, and we were diverted."

Siebrands and her copilot dropped off the operations folks in Victoria, British Columbia.

"We didn't have time to pick up a rescue swimmer," she says. "We flew straight there."

When they arrived, the crewmember in back dropped the basket. "One man was finally able to get in," she says, "but it was clear the other wouldn't be able to maneuver himself into the basket.

"Everything is time related. That's what was the driving factor. These men had been in the water before we were called and were ready to fade away.

"I didn't make the decision until I told the copilot he had the helicopter, and went to the back and saw the situation. Jumping into the water isn't something I'd choose to do, but I couldn't ask anyone else to do it."

She jumped.

"It wasn't until I was in the water that I realized how difficult it was," she says. "Rescue swimmers have masks and snorkels so that they can see and breathe. Being underneath a helicopter hovering over the water, the rotor wash is pretty overwhelming."

The flight mechanic on the helicopter remembers the rescue.

"I looked down at her in the water," he says, "and she was almost past the point of exhaustion."

"The guy was too heavy to put in the basket," Siebrands remembers. "He was totally unconscious. I got into the basket myself and pulled him on top of me, and my copilot hovered us over to a mudflat. Someone had called an ambulance from Forks, and so the crewman and I did CPR until the ambulance arrived."

Hours later, the man died.

"Is there anything we could have done quicker, could have done better?" she asks in a Coast Guard Channel interview.[3]

"We gave him everything we had, all the resources we had," the flight mechanic reports.

Despite initial threats of disciplinary action from the Coast Guard, Siebrands was awarded the United States Coast Guard medal for remarkable initiative, fortitude, and daring in spite of extreme personal danger.

"Later the Coast Guard put a policy in place that you couldn't do what I did," she says with a laugh.

Siebrands exemplifies the willingness to take on challenge and to seize opportunity—to literally jump into opportunity. She didn't start out with her path plotted or planned. Siebrands's story illustrates that having a strategic vision and a long-term perspective on your career should never take away from seizing the chance to turn in an outstanding performance in the moment.

Building Your Risk Tolerance

Experience is critical to building your risk tolerance, but it doesn't immunize you from fear. The willingness to take risks is important throughout your life and career. In other words, facing the wind is not just for takeoff. It's also for full flight.

One of the first women to fly in the Navy is Jane O'Dea, who, like Siebrands, grew up in the Iowa countryside. O'Dea says the biggest risk she took was made *more* difficult because she had already established herself. She didn't only risk failure but also her hard-earned reputation—and, in this specific circumstance, her life as well.

"I always wanted to be a pilot," O'Dea says, "but little girls didn't dream of being pilots in the sixties." Still, she admits that "I was a rough-and-tumble girl growing up." Both of her parents raised O'Dea and her sister to be tough in the face of the neighborhood bullies, and she attributes that to developing the grit she brought with her through her life.

O'Dea planned to go to law school, but when she heard that the Navy might open flight training to women, she signed up right away. She was sent to Newport, Rhode Island, for Women's Officer School (WOS).

"I figured if I wasn't selected [for flight training], I'd get out of Iowa for a few years and finance law school through the GI Bill," she says. Four women, including O'Dea, were selected for flight training. Three graduated, earning their wings in Corpus Christi, Texas, in 1974.

Despite earning their wings, the women pilots were not allowed to carrier qualify as part of their training, though it was required of all the male pilots. This exclusion wasn't the only indication of challenges ahead. O'Dea had heard another warning back in WOS.

"The commander, a pioneer in her own right, was excited for me but cautioned me to be careful, saying, 'The Navy does not reward pioneers.' She was right."

In the midst of her first assignment, O'Dea realized that she was expecting a child. That revelation, and not her exceptional performance, prompted a two-page article in the local newspaper including a quote from her commander saying, "her pregnancy has probably complicated her personal and career life more than it has made problems for me." O'Dea continued her mission in both family and flying. Then, when O'Dea was halfway through her career as a field-grade officer, an unexpected opportunity materialized.

"As a lieutenant commander I was given the opportunity to carrier qualify on the USS *Lexington*," O'Dea says.

It was a big gamble. "I already had a perfectly good reputation as a pilot," O'Dea says. "I risked losing that if I didn't do so well."

She knew what she was getting herself into. "I'd been exposed to taking off from and landing on a carrier enough having been ship's company for over a year," she says. "I'd seen the good, the bad, and the ugly. I'd watched a cold cat (catapult) shot where something happened and the catapult misfired and the plane dribbled off into the ocean. The possibility of a cold cat was especially scary for the plane I was flying because we didn't have ejection seats, so there was an additional risk."

She pauses as she tells me this story, remembering the cold cat.

"The guy I watched on a cold cat punched out, but he almost died anyway. He landed on the deck of the ship and was almost sucked into the intake of the aircraft waiting to take off behind him. Fortunately several brave sailors jumped onto his parachute and saved him."

It wasn't only the danger of a carrier landing itself that worried O'Dea. "I was worried I could let my dad down, too," she says, referring to her career Navy father.

"Do I follow a lifelong dream? Or should I play it safe and say no, I don't want to take this risk?"

O'Dea went for it. "It was very scary, very intense," she says.

A normal runway has thousands of feet for takeoff. On the USS *Lexington*, O'Dea had two hundred feet. The first time she went off the ship, "I looked back once we were in the air, and the ship looked like a postage stamp," she says.

The carrier landing was the biggest challenge. "You have to learn to fly the Fresnel lens," she says, discussing the specific difficulties of navigating at high speeds onto the ship. "There is a row of green lights on either side of a yellow or red light. This is referred to as the meatball. It goes up and down depending on whether you are above or below glide slope. If it turns from yellow to red, you are way below glide slope."

That isn't the only difficulty. In order to maximize space on the carrier, the deck of the USS *Lexington* was angled ten degrees to the left.

"With a fixed runway you correct for crosswinds, but the runway doesn't move," O'Dea says, "but on a carrier you have to keep correcting because the runway is drifting away from you and you have to make constant left corrections. It's the skipper's job to keep the wind within ten degrees of the nose of the ship. Carrier landings require you to put your life completely in someone else's hands."

Because the USS *Lexington* was a smaller, World War II–era carrier with a shorter runway, O'Dea had additional landing requirements.

"We had to do what they call a blue-water cut," O'Dea says, "bringing our throttles to idle while still over the ocean. I looked down at the water while bringing my throttles to idle, and had to have total faith in that landing signal officer on the deck."

She landed it. "I faced the fear, and lived to tell," she laughs.

O'Dea retired from the Navy as a captain. Her flight suit hangs on display at Naval Air Station Pensacola.

After a career in uniform, O'Dea reminds aspiring leaders that "the uniform doesn't make the person wearing it. Performance is everything. Nothing will be given to you. Unfortunately, you will have to work harder and be as good as if not better than your male counterparts to prove yourself."

Finding Your Confidence

Risk-taking requires confidence. Confidence comes from experience, from a track record of successes, but it doesn't always come naturally, especially if you are working in a field that may be resistant to your being there.

Anne Kreamer, author of *Risk/Reward*, writes about the reasons leaders so often shy away from taking risks, attributing the aversion to a psychological desire for stability.

"We are wired to resist giving up the known for the unknown," she writes in *Harvard Business Review*. "None of us tolerates ambiguity well—particularly when the losses and gains underpin our livelihoods or the projected long-term happiness of our families."[4]

At the root of a lack of confidence is fear. Fear is a normal human emotion, and an important one. It is designed to keep us safe from the lions and any modern equivalent on or off the savanna. But fear is an impediment to success, too. As I tell my clients, fear is just a form of resistance. And just like on takeoff, it can be put to use, if we turn toward it and fly directly through it.

In order to be willing to take the necessary risk to move forward, you have to recognize and move through whatever fear might be holding you back. You have to be willing to get uncomfortable, to *be* uncomfortable.

When I spoke at West Point one fall as part of its annual Ethics Conference, the topic of conversation turned to training. Soldiers know that the way you train for push-ups is by doing push-ups, gradually increasing the number of push-ups until you reach your goal. The lesson applies to most anything: You train for grit by doing things requiring grit. You train for courage by doing things that require courage. And you do that by taking smaller risks at first. As you do, you build up your tolerance for uncertainty and your confidence. Over time, it's how you conquer fear.

Alda Siebrands didn't start by jumping out of her own helicopter. She began with an adventure in the Peace Corps. Then she joined the military and asked for opportunities as they arose: Airborne School, Jumpmaster school, flight school. She built up her ability to take risks, and she built up her confidence.

The same goes for Amy McGrath. After multiple instances of raising her hand and taking the hardest and most demanding opportunities while in uniform, she threw her hat in the ring for one of the highest-profile Senate races in the 2020 election cycle.

The willingness to face your fears doesn't ensure smooth sailing. While every environment has its own unique qualities and challenges, studies show consistent problems in the perception of women's performance and abilities because of a number of factors, resulting in often harsh judgment of women who are outstanding performers.

Perhaps the biggest challenge for women in leadership roles is that they are penalized more severely for mistakes, which according to some studies results in less inclination to take the risks necessary for advancement. Other studies don't see the same impact, though they do recognize the penalties women face when they extend themselves. When Catherine Tinsley and Robin Ely studied women's performance compared with that of men in the workplace, they found no significant difference in confidence, willingness to take risks, or other measures commonly assumed to be areas of difference that could point to clear differences in outcomes—namely, fewer women in leadership positions.

"The extent to which employees are able to thrive and succeed at work depends partly on the kinds of opportunities and treatment they receive," Tinsley and Ely write. "People are more likely to behave in ways that undermine their chances for success when they are disconnected from information networks, when they are judged or penalized disproportionately harshly for mistakes or failures, and when they lack feedback. Unfortunately, women are more likely than men to encounter each of these situations."[5]

It is not only in the moment that increased penalties may impact a woman's aversion to risk. Women are also notably reluctant to take riskier stretch assignments, fearing they may not recover from failure and thus cannot afford to take the risks an effective leader needs to take. Research confirms that such concerns are valid: A study by Yale professor Victoria Brescoll and colleagues found that "if women in male-dominated occupations make mistakes, they are accorded less status and seen as less competent than men making the same mistakes."[6]

Growth through Failure

Building your confidence and risk tolerance requires becoming comfortable with failure, or at least learning not to be sidetracked by it. Taking risks means that sometimes you will fail. But it's not failure that matters—it's what you do with it that counts. The difference between leaders who succeed and leaders who don't is that the former see failure as an opportunity to grow.

Carol Dweck, a researcher at Stanford, espouses developing what she calls a growth mindset as opposed to a fixed mindset. People with a fixed mindset tend to run from failures or problems. With a growth mindset, leaders engage with the issue, work on the problem, and find ways to get beyond it. In Dweck's studies, she shows that simply educating children about how trying hard develops new neurons in their brains helps them work through challenges more efficiently.[7] Summed up, her findings are that, "When students believe they can get smarter, they understand that effort makes them stronger. Therefore they put in extra time and effort, and that leads to higher achievement."[8]

Amy McGrath offers an excellent example of a growth mindset when she talks about the benefits of one of her biggest failures. In our conversation, she recounts an incident during her basic course.

"It was night land navigation," she remembers, "and I failed the course. I couldn't find the tire in the middle of the woods. I was sent to remedial training." It was humiliating because, "When you're a woman, everyone knows you failed."

With the wisdom of years, she sees her botched experience at land navigation as fortuitous.

In a subsequent training exercise, "I was the strongest at land nav," she says. "Suddenly I was this valuable member of my team, because of all that extra training I'd had to do. I was the only one who could navigate at night. The failure, and the follow-on training, made me valuable to my squad."

Reflecting on the idea of failure, she laughs.

"There were so many times I failed. So many flights . . . I don't trust someone who hasn't failed. How do you know how they will react?"

In order to be a gritty leader, you need to learn how to operate out of a growth mindset and, when you encounter the inevitable failure, to make a plan to correct course and move forward. Perhaps failure for you is missing out on a promotion or a job you wanted. Perhaps it is losing a deal. Making a bad call. Having a growth mindset doesn't mean that you won't feel the big emotions—grief, shame, and regret—when you do fail, but focusing on next steps forward allows you to use adversity to help you rise.

Lieutenant Colonel Kate Germano experienced this truth firsthand after she was assigned as the commander of a training battalion in the Marine Corps. When she took command, she'd been told that the women in her battalion would either end up crying on her couch or baking cupcakes. Women were segregated in training, and had historically underperformed their male counterparts. Germano decided to make a change. She focused on "making data-driven decisions," and while results improved dramatically, there were those who were unwilling or unable to support the direct leadership she brought to the table. She expresses regret that her direct approach made some women trainees feel that she was unsupportive. Ultimately she was relieved of her command.

"I wanted to kill myself," she says. "It was the worst thing I had ever experienced other than the death of my mom to cancer. I felt an overwhelming sense of shame because of the very personal attacks on my leadership and character in the media, and almost gave up. I was lucky to be surrounded by people who believed in me and prevented me from going over the edge, but ultimately, I wasn't willing to leave this world without knowing the real truth about why I was fired, and how I could have contributed to the problem."

For Germano, the experience of learning from failure was absolutely essential to developing and drawing on grit.

"Grit is a combination of seeing mistakes as stepping stones on the path to self-realization rather than bridge burners," she says, "and having the determination and self-compassion after you fail to try again."

Her experience helped her connect to purpose in the midst of incredible difficulty.

"I set out on a journey of self-discovery and personal growth, which helped me bounce back," Germano continues. "While I learned more about my personal flaws than I ever wanted to know, over time, I realized that being fired as a leader does not equate to necessarily being a bad human. I was able to start seeing it as just one event in my life, rather than a reflection of bad character. By doing a lot of research on the social and neuroscience related to fear of change, self-compassion, and emotional intelligence, I came to understand that human beings aren't born with fixed levels of empathy and self-awareness, but that we can carefully cultivate and grow these aspects of our hearts and minds if we are willing to change."

Germano's dedication to personal growth in the wake of failure helped her work to rectify aspects of Marine Corps training that put women at a disadvantage.

I relate to the acuity of Germano's experience. The most difficult time I had finding grit in my years in service—the times it was hardest for me to face the wind—was when confronting my own failure.

As a young officer, I'd worked long, hard days, weeks, and months. I'd earned top ratings on my evaluations. After leading my first platoon, I took a second platoon to Bosnia.

Halfway through the deployment in Bosnia, our battalion of Apaches had the opportunity to fire a gunnery at Glamoc, a firing range in the western part of the country with an ancient name drawn either from the word *sheep*, referencing the shepherding common in the area, or from *rocky hills*, an apt description of the landscape. Qualifying on the Apache's weapons systems was an annual requirement, and highly anticipated. Not only was it a challenge, it was fun, and came with a usually friendly sense of competition as crews vied for the title of company "Top Gun." We started working toward the week we would spend away, looking at tents and cots, inventorying mechanics kits, and planning the flight. A day before we were scheduled to launch from Comanche Base to fly west, I heard from another pilot that my platoon instructor pilot wasn't feeling well. I sought him out at the flight line.

"How are you doing, Chuck?" I asked.

Chuck was a gentle man with a soft Texas accent, never one for raising his voice or making a fuss.

"Oh, I'm all right, LT," he said.

"I heard you weren't feeling well," I said.

"Oh, it's not too bad,"

"You know we can fill your seat if you'd rather not fly tomorrow," I offered.

"No, no, it'll all be OK," he said.

"OK," I said. "But it's easy to make a crew change, so keep me posted, OK?"

He agreed.

The next morning, our flight crews walked to the flight line and took off in a flight of nine, our eight company helicopters and a Black Hawk. The terrain fell away behind us, forested mountains and hills giving way to high desert. It was an easy daytime flight, little threat in the area and a gunnery to look forward to, as well as a change from our routine at the tiny Comanche Base West. Spirits were high.

We landed in Glamoc, and arranged the aircraft to face a line of cliffs where targets had been prepared for us to engage in the days to follow.

Each crew shut down their aircraft and carried duffel bags and flight gear to the company tents. After unloading, I headed over to the tactical operations center (TOC). I ran into our company instructor pilot (IP) on the way.

"LT!" he called, waving me down. I stopped and waited for him.

"Chuck's not doing well. He's bleeding out of both ends."

We hurried to the TOC and arranged for a medical evacuation flight (medevac) to take Chuck back to Comanche Base. (The doctor there immediately transported him to a hospital in Germany.)

Once Chuck was loaded onto the medevac, our company IP, whose name was George, came back to talk to me.

"LT," he said, "you've got to take care of your people."

I bristled, believing myself firmly committed to that end.

"I agree, George. I asked Chuck how he was and whether or not he wanted to go," I replied, defensively. "I told him we could fill his seat."

George looked at me.

"LT, sometimes you have to take care of your people when they don't know how to take care of themselves," he said.

I swallowed hard, chastened. I knew that I had failed. I had failed the key leadership precept I believed to my core, one I had internalized after early mistakes, with good guidance, and still I'd made the wrong decision, one affecting the well-being of one of my pilots, about whom I cared deeply.

There was nothing more to do. I wanted only to find a quiet place and nurse my wounds, which were the worst kind—self-inflicted, and a result of my own mistakes.

But there was no quiet, private place. There rarely is in the Army, and never on deployment. I had a week of gunnery ahead of me. I was accountable to my backseater for my best perfor-mance. I had to lead my platoon, anticipate and respond to what their requirements might be. There was no time to sulk.

This is where grit was hardest to access: in the face of my own failings. These experiences where I failed, and the resulting shame, were always the most difficult places to maneuver.

In Glamoc, once the medevac lifted off from the ground, I had to accept a measure of humility while still moving forward with what was required of me. I didn't know everything I needed to know to be a good leader. I had thought I was putting my people first, but I hadn't been careful enough.

I wish I could say I learned everything I needed to learn that time and that everything became easier and smoother, and that I became wiser, but this was far from the only mistake I made in or out of uniform.

As someone who has stumbled painfully many times, I can tell you there is only one solution to it: when you fall, you pick your-self back up and move forward. The first few steps aren't always straight, but you take those shaky steps anyway. You reconnect to your own core purpose, decide what you will do differently the next time, and focus on your goal.

Getting back up and moving forward makes you stronger and grittier. Internalizing the lesson makes you better. Applying what you learned to how you do things going forward is how you be-come a better leader.

Strong leaders look at fear as just another form of resistance—something they can turn toward and move through, and that perspective emboldens them to take risks that could well lead to failure. As Eleanor Roosevelt said: "You gain strength, courage, and confidence by every experience in which you really stop to look fear in the face." With every incremental experience that pushes you to grow, you gain confidence for even greater chal-lenges ahead.

Learning from Failure

1. After failing to pay close enough attention to the signals from one of my pilots, I learned that I needed to be more careful, and more willing to take action to help my soldiers even when they resisted. Consider a time when you failed in the past. What lessons did you learn from the experience? How were you able to take that learning to change how you approached the next challenge?

2. How can you find a way to celebrate risk-taking and even failure in your team? One suggestion is to implement an occasional award for an initiative that fails, or another form of recognition for trying new things, regardless of the outcome. What else comes to mind?

3. Sharing stories of overcoming disappointments or what came of a failure is one way to encourage innovation in a team, while also encouraging candor and humility. Can you find a way to share the story of your own failures and what you learned from them with your team or colleagues?

— 7 —

Have the Audacity to Be Yourself

"One's real life is so often the life that one does not lead."

—Oscar Wilde

"And this above all: to thine own self be true.
And it must follow, as the night the day, thou
canst not then be false to any man."

—William Shakespeare

As young officers, Major General Dee McWilliams and her husband were stationed in Germany. The stress of work requirements and living overseas led them to the difficult though amicable decision to part ways. McWilliams took leave to go back to the States to settle her affairs, and then returned to Germany. Her first day back on duty, she found her newly unmarried status had changed how she was perceived. She reported to her commander, who closed the door to his office, and then vulgarly propositioned her.

"He leaned back in his chair, looked over his desk at me, and patted the front of his pants," she says. Then he said, "There's no padlock on this zipper."

Her response?

"I opened the office door, which led into a room of ten civilians and officers working at their desks, and said, 'You know what this guy just told me? He told me there was no padlock on his zipper.'"

She walked away and went back to work, and back to her career.

In over twenty-nine years of service in the Army, McWilliams commanded four companies and a training battalion. She taught leadership and served as director of military personnel management for the Department of the Army. And while she was shattering barriers in her career, she never let the requirements of the job take over who she was as a person. She knew inherently that her success required authenticity.

Rebecca Newton, management professor at the London School of Economics, suggests that authenticity goes hand in hand with adaptability (a topic we'll consider in chapter 8). While those two characteristics may seem at odds, they can be complementary. As Newton points out, we can adapt how we work and relate to others while still remaining true to our own core values. McWilliams was able to make the two aspects of leadership work together from the first moment she put on a uniform.

When McWilliams joined the Army, in 1974, she was commissioned into the Women's Army Corps and sent to Fort McClellan for training.

"It was training for lady officers," she recalls. "We learned the history and structure of the WAC and of the Army. We learned how to do correspondence. We were not allowed to be photographed in fatigues. We could not touch a weapon."

After completing her training, McWilliams remembers, she requested an assignment in the Adjutant General's (AG) Corps, the military branch responsible for personnel administration. "I figured degrees in sociology and psychology qualified me for that work," she remembers.

The woman making assignments had other ideas. "I'm going to put you down for Air Defense Artillery," she told McWilliams. "Your husband is in Air Defense. That would be cute."

McWilliams did not find it cute and was willing to say so.

She retorted, "Ma'am, is that the way you make Army assignments? Because you think something is cute?" Her resistance was effective. She walked away with an assignment to AG at Fort Harrison, Indiana.

During McWilliams's assignment at Fort Harrison, women officers were given the opportunity, but were not required, to qualify on the M16 rifle and the .45 pistol. One woman opted out. McWilliams wouldn't have it. "Do you realize that you're giving all the guys in the class the idea that a woman can't do something?" she asked her fellow female officer.

The woman decided to try shooting after all.

McWilliams is up front about her candor.

"I figured if I didn't fit into the Army, they could throw me out and I could go do something else." This attitude, she says, gave her "the room to be creative"—in other words, she was able to be herself. She was able to adapt.

Being yourself in a culture that may seem to demand something different is not easy for most of us, even the leaders I interviewed for this book, which is why McWilliams's story is such a standout. It was not easy for me. But being yourself is an important component of grit.

The courage to stay true to yourself requires many things, including speaking out against something you don't believe in. This certainly doesn't come as naturally to everyone as it did for McWilliams. Many women I interviewed spoke with regret about times they could—and should—have spoken out.

Colleen Farrell served on one of the Marine Corps Female Engagement Teams (FETs), which conducted cultural outreach, civil affairs, and civil-stability operations in support of special-operations work in Afghanistan. Farrell's team operated out of Forward Operating Base Delaram in southern Afghanistan, in the volatile Helmand Province.

Farrell was raised a Quaker, and the importance of service ran deep. That propensity for service combined with her athletic background—playing basketball, baseball, and field hockey in high school and field hockey through college as well—led her toward the military. After college, she and her sister enrolled together in the Marine Corps Officer Candidate School (OCS) in Quantico, Virginia.

The sisters were not able to finish their training. Their mother, who had multiple sclerosis, had taken a turn for the worse. Both returned home, and their mother passed away two weeks later.

Colleen and her sister decided to go back to OCS. That fall, they returned to the next course, and completed it. Later Farrell would join the FET and deploy. But it was her early experience as a young officer that she looks back on with regret.

"When I started at the Basic School, the six-month course that teaches brand-new lieutenants the knowledge and leadership required to be a rifle-platoon commander, I wanted to fit in with my new community of peers and I wanted to excel," she says. "Half of our training consisted of classroom instruction. My company, comprised of two hundred brand-new lieutenants, of which only ten were women, would pile ourselves into one classroom for ten hours a day and listen to instructors lecture about the basics of infantry, artillery, and air-support tactics. We were often asked questions throughout the lectures, and inevitably one lieutenant would shoot their hand up, spring to the position of attention, and shout out the answer. Every single time a female lieutenant would answer a question, my peers around me would mock her in a nasally tone. And I would laugh because that was what was expected of me in that culture.

"Only years later did I realize that my acceptance and compliance with this behavior kept me from ever answering a single question myself, as I knew I would be mocked like all the other females who dared to exhibit their knowledge. Not only did I show my peers it was acceptable to treat others this way by remaining silent, I perpetuated the belief that this behavior was funny.

"Later in my military career, I took time to reflect," she continues. "I thought about those times where I said nothing and did nothing when sexist comments were made, making me complicit. Specifically, I thought back to my years of Quaker education where equality is one of our core beliefs. The Marine Corps taught me to lead by example, and to me that means remembering your values and trying to live by them every day. I had overlooked so many opportunities to speak up to my peers and superiors about such comments and attitudes because I wasn't fully living my values and letting my life speak."

Farrell understood only later how much she had compromised her own values by not speaking up when it mattered, and that the slights that she saw played out every day were not as insignificant as she was wont to believe.

Even McWilliams admits that it takes bravery to speak up. When she and I speak about grit, she tells me that the greatest growth opportunity for women leaders is "the audacity to be yourself."

Audacity is defined as the willingness to take bold risks. Even if judged only by their willingness to put on a uniform, the women I interviewed for this book have audacity in spades. Successfully maneuvering in environments while remaining authentic requires extreme audacity. Accessing that audacity isn't necessarily automatic, especially for women in situations where they are in the minority. It's a journey, one that can be fostered by three distinctive steps: bridging the confidence gap, turning down the noise, and taking ownership of who you are and the work you do.

Bridging the Confidence Gap

Katty Kay and Claire Shipman, authors and news anchors for ABC and BBC News, respectively, described "the confidence gap" in a May 2014 article in *The Atlantic*.[1] They exposed the seemingly irrational insecurities many top women carry around with them. Despite such impressive accomplishments as degrees from top universities, lead positions in industry, or mastery of multiple languages, some women still assume they are incompetent. Both Kay and Shipman admitted to assuming that men who were direct and outspoken were more competent than they were. They are far from alone.

In their seminal 1978 paper on this lack of confidence despite expertise, clinical psychologists Pauline R. Clance and Suzanne A. Imes called this phenomenon "the imposter syndrome," and acknowledged that many more women than men fall victim to it.[2] This confidence gap between men and women matters because it limits women's ability to achieve and fight for equal pay and job status. It can prevent you from raising your hand for challenging assignments—especially when others in your organization demonstrate a confidence misunderstood as competence, as is typical in mostly male environments. In short, the confidence gap interferes with being yourself, which in turn inhibits your ability to make your best contributions.

Lieutenant Colonel Tammy Barlette, one of the first women to fly the A-10 Warthog in the Air Force and later a fighter-pilot instructor and drone pilot, remembers suppressing her own contributions because of being impressed with the confidence of her male counterparts.

Barlette had been deployed to Korea for her first assignment in the A-10 and had struggled with confidence, despite the fact that her performance had never given her reason to doubt her abilities. "Then one day—I remember the day very clearly—I looked around and realized all the guys were just faking their confidence."

Barlette continues, "I was in the vault, the area in the squadron where the classified materials are kept, studying, when the weapons officer walked in the door and threw out a question to the group of us studying there. I knew the answer but paused to be certain. Before I spoke up one of the guys confidently blurted out an answer. I knew it was not the answer and said to him, 'That's not right.'

"I sat there for a moment, shocked as I realized that that's what the guys had been doing all along—faking it. I had wondered why I felt like I didn't know as much as the guys, but never realized that they approached this environment differently than I. I had always felt like being confident in an answer I wasn't sure of was borderline lying. Although it still felt slightly inauthentic, I knew it was a tactic I needed to try. I realized the guys were often answering from their gut. Even if they weren't absolutely certain, they were just spitting out their answer with confidence. It completely shifted the way I went forward from that point. I remember making the decision from that point on that if I was asked a question and an answer popped into my head, I wasn't going to hold back. I was just going to spit it out with confidence."

Barlette made a conscious effort to stop her self-doubt when it occurred, forcing herself to answer with authority in the moment.

"It was really, really hard at first," she continues. "But it blew my mind to realize that about 90 percent of the time the answer that popped into my head was correct. I realized the guys were carrying around an armor of confidence that I hadn't been carrying. Putting on that armor of outer confidence made a significant impact on my inner confidence moving forward with my career."

Barlette went on to successfully complete the notoriously difficult US Air Force Weapons School, an accomplishment she
could only have earned with her newfound surety.

Ultimately, it's up to each of us to decide that we are qualified
enough. This decision comes in large part from the work we've already covered in this book: knowing your story, having an understanding of your core purpose, and having a dream team in place
that can remind you of the value you bring to the table in those
moments when you most doubt it.

The final piece of bridging the confidence gap comes from understanding and owning your uniqueness—what makes you different from the others. That's how you can ensure that your actions and reactions remain consistent with your character even in
the face of new and possibly hostile environments and challenges.
From the most junior to the most senior leaders I interviewed for
this book, the message is clear: despite the difficulty, it is critical
for a leader to remain true to who she is. As Eleanor Roosevelt
said: "Remember always that you have not only a right to be an
individual, you have an obligation to be one."

Carol Gallagher, who holds a doctorate in organizational
behavior and is often consulted for her research on executive
women, interviewed nearly two hundred women executives for
her bestselling *Going to the Top.* Among other findings from her
study is the importance of operating from a place of deep authenticity, in part because of authenticity's significance in how
we connect to others.

"You can't build genuine relationships based on what you
think people want you to be," she writes. "It's powerful and effective for a woman to be herself."[3]

Of course, true authenticity is more challenging than it seems
and than it ought to be. Women in the military, and in any male-
dominated field or culture, are forced to work through what
Stanford law professor Deborah Rhode described in 2001 as a
"double standard and a double bind," avoiding being seen as "too

soft or too strident, too aggressive or not aggressive enough."[4] Women are culturally expected to have relationships as their primary focus, but leaders are expected to be task-driven—this is the double bind, making it very difficult for women to succeed in leadership positions.

Social scientists have found that some women succeed in navigating this double bind by adopting an androgynous identity. But other researchers suggest that in many cases, or in particularly male institutions, androgyny may not be enough. In these examples, women may choose to adopt a more masculine set of leadership characteristics.[5] Both indicate adaptability to the extreme, but at the expense of authenticity.

Women who do become more aggressive—either out of necessity or out of their own tendencies—are often penalized for this assertiveness. Pew Research data indicates that 74 percent of adults see being assertive as beneficial to men, and only 50 percent believe it helps women. Twenty-three percent of adults believe assertiveness hurts women in politics, compared with only 5 percent believing the same about men.[6]

Being one of the guys rarely felt comfortable to even the toughest women I interviewed for this book. Most found that trying to be someone they weren't or acting in a way inconsistent with their values and identity only hindered their grit, because the psychological toll made navigating the double bind even harder.

When Tammy Barlette arrived at pilot training, she initially tried hard to fit into the pilot culture.

"When I first got to pilot training, I felt like I had to be a guy," she says. "I had to be aggressive. I had to talk like they did, really push the limits not just on flying and academics but life. Not only was it uncomfortable for me, but I watched other women try to step into this manly role and it didn't look natural. I started to realize I didn't need to be like that."

At the same time, it would have been naive not to understand the specifics of fighter-pilot culture. Barlette acknowledges that it was still important to work within the environment of a fighter squadron.

"At work I was more emotionally masculine. I kept my feelings to myself, and that's good for the environment. It's the way you need to be."

Where Barlette learned the importance of being true to herself came in interactions outside of work.

"When I first started out, I'd put on my 'tough guy' facade and go out drinking with the guys. I tried talking like them, even though it wasn't me," she tells me. "Eventually, I defaulted back to just being my authentic self, and not only was it much more enjoyable to just be me, I discovered that that's what the guys wanted—to get to know *me*, not who I thought they wanted me to be.

"As I got older, and wiser," she continues, "the conversations with my male counterparts matured as well, and they'd say, 'Yeah, we don't want you ladies to try and be like a guy. We want you to be you. You do the job, you do it well, but be yourself.' That hit home."

Many of the leaders I interviewed weren't as fortunate as Barlette, and because of how they perceived the requirements of their job, they spent years functioning in a way that ran counter to who they were.

"Lucky" Heather Penney, the retired Air National Guard F-16 pilot whom you met back in chapter 3, is as gritty as they come, and she is candid about the pressure to fit into an organization that embraces hypermasculinity as a shared value.

"Those traditions and rituals we have that are hypermasculine and sexualized have nothing to do with actually making the team better at what we do, or more mission effective at what we do," she says. "They don't create higher performance or esprit de corps. Esprit de corps comes from the organization that works hard, has mutual respect and trust for each other, and is a high-performing organization. It has nothing to do with whether or not you go to the strip club that night. But there was no one to teach me those lessons, to teach me that. So for a long time as a young fighter pilot I had to pretend that all that was OK. Internalizing behaviors and actions that ran against my core beliefs and values was extremely disorienting. It actually took my squadron commander to teach me that it wasn't appropriate or acceptable."

Penney goes on to describe an experience at a flight briefing for the squadron's pilots.

"We were in the middle of a mass briefing, and in between each section popped up a hardcore porn picture," she says. "At the end of the mass brief I said, 'Hey, great briefing guys!' I wasn't going to rock the boat.

"Not only did the commander tell all the guys it was inappropriate and that it would never happen again," she continues, "but he told me that I shouldn't have to tolerate things like that, and he apologized. It was a real wake-up moment for me. That was my clue that Wow, I don't have to pretend that these behaviors that I find personally demoralizing and disrespectful are OK. The hypersexual locker-room rituals only served to highlight what an outsider I was.

"Women are incentivized not only to not be feminine, but to be like the guys," she says. "It also means you can't affiliate with other women. Some women tried to out-guy the guys to prove that they belonged. I did a little of that myself."

Finding a way to stay true to yourself and your own values is the only sustainable way to find success. Nowhere was this more apparent than at West Point when women first started attending, a crucible in the extreme.

Carol Barkalow, who matriculated in the first class of women at West Point, wrote in 1990 that "West Point is perhaps one of the few remaining places in late-twentieth century America built on the belief that outer images are sincerely expected to reflect inner truths. That they seldom do, and that the place lives on in spite of it, is both the miracle and the tragedy of the Academy."[7]

Women's entry into these bastions of male dominion would have been difficult on its own. The integration was made more so by the timing of President Ford's 1975 bill permitting women to enter the service academies, which went into effect in the wake of a West Point cheating scandal. At the same time, cadets were reeling from the departure of the Academy's superintendent, who resigned after an investigation revealed his involvement in covering up the My Lai massacre.

"Undeniably," writes Barkalow, "the Academy believed itself to be under attack and felt compelled, once more, as it had at other times during its 174 years, to justify its very existence."

A number of male officers had publicly opposed admitting women to the academies before the women's arrival. And while all cadets faced hazing, "men had to prove themselves weak before they became subject to this [special hazing]; women had to prove themselves strong before they were spared it," writes Barkalow.

The environment women entered early in the days of integration at West Point and the other academies was far from receptive.

"In my naïveté," one cadet interviewed for Barkalow's book recalls, "I thought, they've passed a law, of course they'll welcome us."

While still a cadet herself, Barkalow recognized what would emerge as a common piece of advice from those successful in integrating into an all-male field, which might be true of integration into any group. She wrote in her diary on February 8, 1978:

"I got a letter from a friend today who said: Why the Army? She said she couldn't imagine joining up because she was too independent. How can I tell her that I'm very independent, and that independence is a state of mind? That's the trouble with so many cadets—they lose themselves in the system. As long as you stay in touch with who you really are inside, you'll have no problem with West Point. I'm keeping my individuality."[8]

Aristotle writes about eudaimonia, often simplistically defined as happiness, but more accurately considered to be a state of well-being or flourishing. Key in its very definition (according to Richard M. Ryan and Edward L. Deci, clinical-psychology researchers who authored a seminal paper on eudaimonia) is being real: ". . . well-being is not so much an outcome or end state as it is a process of fulfilling or realizing one's daimon or true nature—that is, of fulfilling one's virtuous potentials and living as one was inherently intended to live."[9]

This requirement for individual authenticity works in a virtuous circle: It takes courage to be yourself, and—as Harvard Business School professor and expert on organizational psychology Francesca Gino advises—being authentic helps develop your courage.[10]

Gino has demonstrated that reconnecting to your core values through a simple writing exercise increases your willingness to speak up even when something might be controversial. (I will include instructions for this exercise at the end of the chapter.) Grounding yourself in your core purpose gives you an extra measure of confidence and determination. Without this rootedness—this connection to your authentic self—you'll operate from a place that is much more tenuous. With it, you stabilize your platform and ensure the most powerful foundation for the difficult work of leadership. It is how you connect to grit even in those moments when you may be doubting your own abilities.

The second element toward leading with authenticity is more tactical. Remaining connected to your true self requires reducing the static and blocking out the other voices that may be undermining your confidence.

Turn Down the Noise

On the opening pages of this book, I shared the story of that early mission in Bosnia as a part of the NATO Stabilization Force in support of the Dayton Peace Accords. On this flight, we were flying an armed aerial reconnaissance of heavy weapons storage sites under infrared. The days were hot then, the nights cool. We easily navigated under a clear infrared picture to the location where we would conduct the reconnaissance.

As we slowed to a high hover, the voice of the radar warning system came through my helmet: we were being tracked by the most lethal antiaircraft system in the world.

My backseater asked: "What do you want me to do, LT? Do you want me to break the hard deck?"

As soon as he asked the question, the sound in our helmets changed: now the system had acquired our aircraft as a target. The weapon system had locked on. It could fire at will. I called up the controlling agency to report the signal. They soon came back on the radio.

"If you're nervous, return to base, but don't break the hard deck."

I had a decision to make, the consequences of which could be life or death. In a few seconds, I considered what we knew: I knew tracking and acquisition by this antiaircraft weapon system was against the rules of engagement. I knew that there had been no recent hostile engagements at this level, so provocation was more likely than engagement. I knew that responding with hostility would generate international attention.

I reached over to the threat-radar warning system and turned down the volume. I turned down the noise. We continued the mission without incident.

I think of this story as an example of how difficult it is to manage the many inputs we have at any given time. The noise you're hearing probably isn't a threat-radar warning system. More likely it has to do with other people's demands or perhaps their unfair perceptions or other negativity. Sometimes the noise you have to turn down is coming from within your circle, from people who want only the best for you but are not supporting your work or your goals. Maybe it is coming from openly hostile sources. Perhaps the noise is the cacophony of too many demands: meetings, phone calls, conferences, emails, text messages, deadlines. As overwhelming as too much information can be, the negativity from other sources can be deadly.

When Katie Higgins, the first woman to fly with the Blue Angels, pushed herself to take on new opportunities, she found herself bombarded by signals antagonistic to her vision and her success from both peers and family members. Navigating these inputs successfully while working toward her goals required grit and tactical decision making.

Higgins was already well acquainted with the military after growing up as the daughter of a Navy F/A-18 pilot, moving with her family every two or three years and even spending her first two years of high school in Yokosuka, Japan. The military legacy in Higgins's family was strong. Her paternal great-grandparents had emigrated from Sweden, and her grandfather, believing in the idea of giving back to their new country, served during World War II, Korea, and Vietnam.

"He really instilled in me the idea of a life of service," Higgins says.

All three men in her father's family had attended military academies, so Higgins applied to all three, was given her choice, and chose the Navy.

"I'd thought I wanted to be a fighter pilot like my dad," she says, "but throughout my time at school I fell in love with the Marine Corps. I was so impressed with the caliber of enlisted Marines, and the loyalty, hard work, and dedication of the officers to their subordinates. I wanted to be a part of that organization." Higgins' interest was not well received.

When Higgins put in her request for an assignment in the United States Marine Corps, many of her Naval Academy classmates harassed her.

"'Ol' Chesty Puller would be rolling over in his grave if he knew she was a Marine,'" Higgins remembers a classmate at the Naval Academy saying when she was selected for the Marine

Corps, a reference to the most decorated Marine in US history. "If I had to work with her I'd throw a grenade in her tent," said another.

"It was hurtful, mean shit," she says. "When I went to TBS [the Basic School] I had a staff company commander tell me that the only reason I would survive in the USMC is because they could teach a monkey to fly."

Despite the criticism, Higgins trained as a pilot in the C-130. In the middle of her second combat deployment as a young officer—the deployment following her experiences flying Harvest Hawk, which I shared in chapter 2—she received an unexpected call from the elite Blue Angels demonstration squadron inviting her to apply. With this new opportunity came new resistance. Offensive comments erupted from colleagues and their family members.

The comments stung, but Higgins refused to be deterred.

Though young and still junior in rank, with two combat deployments under her belt and the requisite flight hours, Higgins met the requirements to apply. She put her name in for assessment with the Blue Angels. She tried out and was accepted as their first female pilot.

Higgins' advice comes from hard-earned experience. "Don't let other people define your self-confidence," she advises. "Be open to constructive criticism, because officers should always be looking to better themselves, but if someone is trying to tear you down just to be a jerk, move on with your life."

Higgins is expressing a core truth. She's also describing a skill fundamental to operating with grit and being yourself: the ability to turn down the noise when it does not support you and your goals. Too much noise is overwhelming. Negativity is toxic. No matter what the source of the external input, it's critical to tune out those things that don't support your work.

When you turn down the noise, you create more space to hear your own voice—that unique combination of what you know to be true based on your experience, your values, and your core purpose.

How do you turn down the noise? Checking in with your dream team is one way, and focusing on what comes from their recommendations. Reconnecting to your core purpose and your values is another, perhaps by revisiting the exercises you did earlier in this book or by other reading that supports your focus. Deciding which inputs you will consider and which you will not is important. Stay focused on the information that matters and continue to move forward.

Taking ownership of your decisions is yet another, and perhaps the most powerful, way to build trust in your own decision making.

Taking Ownership

When I was a new platoon leader, the crew chief for my Apache, tail number 248, was Specialist Mike Cameron. Cameron wasn't responsible for any people, or for anything other than the basic maintenance of the helicopter. He rarely smiled, though he was well liked by his fellow crew chiefs.

What I remember most about Cameron was this: an utter reliability, not only to get the job done, but to perform it well in excess of the standards expected of him. Though our battalion worked long hours—over days, weeks, and months—Cameron never complained. He may have grimaced once or twice, but he focused on excellent work. Cameron didn't talk behind people's backs, or grouse with other enlisted soldiers about the amount of work expected of them. He did his job, and then more.

I remember one flight in particular when Cameron came out to launch the aircraft. Crew chiefs were expected to be present at launch with hearing and eye protection, standing just outside the arc of the rotor blades and holding a fire extinguisher. What

I remember is coming out to preflight and seeing that Cameron had already untied the aircraft and opened up the panels necessary for our inspection, something I never saw another crew chief do. My copilot and I performed our inspection and closed the panels. We put on our vests and climbed into the cockpit. As we began the run-up procedure, Cameron came back up to the aircraft and opened the transmission door, watching as the rotors came to full RPM. He was checking to be sure nothing was leaking on the transmission deck.

His exceptional engagement and willingness to take the initiative across and beyond the full spectrum of his responsibility taught me what leadership and ownership should and could look like. Cameron was the shining star of our platoon, and it wasn't long before he was known throughout the company and across the battalion.

Specialist Sue Harris, the only female crew chief I ever had, is another example. Harris was a tiny thing, perhaps five feet tall, and a bundle of focused energy. She embodied all of the traits of the leaders we've already discussed, exceeding expectations in every way. On her physical fitness test, she "super-maxed" even the male standards, performing 120 perfect push-ups and sit-ups in the allotted two-minute timeframe every single time.

But the circumstance I remember most about Harris came while we were on deployment to Bosnia. The crew chiefs both maintained the aircraft and pulled security shifts in security towers positioned around the perimeter of our base at Tuzla West. These were twenty-four-hour shifts. After soldiers pulled a security shift, they had allotted time off to rest and recover.

Harris was the crew chief assigned to the aircraft I was scheduled to fly one evening, right in the middle of her time off after pulling security. That night, as my backseater and I walked out onto the flight line to preflight, Harris came running after us.

"What are you doing, Harris?" I asked. "You're supposed to be resting!"

"You're in my aircraft, Ma'am, and I'm going to be there when you launch," Harris replied with the broad smile she was known for.

Her presence was not required, but she had such ownership of her job and her aircraft that she couldn't bear missing a launch.

"The instinct of ownership is fundamental in man's nature," said nineteenth-century philosopher William James. Ownership is a key part of a leader's makeup, and critical to grit. Perhaps the most powerful lesson of ownership is that it does not depend on rank or position. Like leadership, ownership is something that can (and should) be exercised by every single person.

Allowing and even expecting individual ownership permits a more decentralized leadership model, giving vitality and originality to the work that needs to be done, as well as protecting it from stalling out or collapsing in the absence of the key leader. Over the course of officer training programs, we were taught that the Western military model emphasized this decentralized leadership. In case of compromised communications or the death or incapacity of a leader, operations could continue on. (There are critics of this idea, both of the degree to which it has been maintained and the desirability of it, and convincing arguments that in the past fifty years the US military has become more centralized than before.) Decentralizing execution, at a minimum, is meant to provide the subordinate or tactical commander room to maneuver, with the understanding that "no plan survives first contact with the enemy." The ability to maneuver in the absence of specific guidance requires a sense of ownership.

Despite William James's proclamation and the clear benefits of individual ownership, across the country and across industries, executives I work with bemoan a lack of ownership in employees. The reason that the examples of Cameron and Harris are so striking is that their acceptance of responsibility and striving for excellence are far from the norm. Many people do not take the initiative. They do not own their work. They criticize those willing to work because it reflects on their unwillingness to take on tasks. This is crippling for the performance of any group, military unit, or corporation. Without employees taking ownership, a culture can rapidly devolve to one of inaction, blame, and disengagement.

The data supports the executives' concerns. In a 2018 Gallup poll, employee engagement was reported at only 34 percent, with 13 percent of employees reporting that they were "actively disengaged."[11] This is actually the *best* performance Gallup has seen since it began reporting this critical figure, showing how far workplaces have to go to maximize employee contributions.

In Francesca Gino's studies, a powerful correlation emerges between ownership and performance. "Ownership," Gino writes, "triggers a 'mindset of possession' that, once activated, persists over various contexts and tasks and influences later choices."[12] Not only does a mindset of possession affect an employee's perspective on her organization, it also makes employees more helpful and generous toward others. Even reminding people of their ownership by prompting them to write a few sentences about something over which they felt ownership increased generosity and good will, according to Gino.

Other research findings concur. In a study of employees at the University of Michigan and the University of Minnesota, results "demonstrated positive links between psychological ownership for the organization and employee attitudes (organizational commitment, job satisfaction, organization-based self-esteem), and work behavior (performance and organizational citizenship)."[13]

Ownership is part of the excitement of leadership. There is a particular thrill in knowing that the success or failure of an operation depends on you—how you've planned and coordinated and brought others along. Leaders are committed to making a difference, and owning an outcome means they have a chance to do exactly that.

The opportunity for ownership must be earned, discovered, and sometimes fought for. Perhaps the most inspiring stories of women who have done that come from those intrepid American female pilots who advocated for the opportunity to fly for their country during World War II.

When Edna Davis was a young woman in Ohio and California in the 1940s, she saved every cent of her eleven-cent-a-week allowance in a can she labeled "flying money." When Davis had enough saved, her mother would drive her to the airfield, where Davis would pay fifty cents for a fifteen-minute ride. Davis heard that the record-setting aviator and businesswoman Jackie Cochran had started the Women Airforce Service Pilots (WASPs), a program employing female pilots in the war effort (though they were barred from flying combat). Davis wrote to Cochran, but never heard back.

How many other stories end with never hearing back and letting an opportunity go? But Davis wasn't about to accept that kind of an ending. She would find another way. Davis owned not just her work, but the very opportunity itself. After not receiving a response from Jackie Cochran, Davis applied to and was accepted into Mills College, where she knew she could join the Civil Air Patrol, eventually finding her way into the WASPs.

"There's a certain percentage of the female population that nobody tells no," she informs me. "I got on the train to [WASP training in] Texas with about six cents in my pocket.

"After I graduated," she continues, "I was sent to Dodge City, Kansas, in the dead of winter to learn how to fly the [twin-engine Martin B-26 Marauder, a medium bomber], which had the worst reputation in the Air Force. It came right from the design table into production to our flight line. Nobody knew its idiosyncrasies. It was dangerous, because nobody knew how to teach anybody else how to fly the airplane."

Davis never let danger dissuade her from pursuing her dream.

She went on to become the first woman to solo in the B-26 Marauder, and she flew the B-26 out of Arlington, Texas, towing targets to help train gunners from around the world.

"I loved it," she says.

Then she recounts one particularly notable flight. "I was towing a target about 250 yards behind our B-26 for a group of Chinese B-24 gunnery trainees who had just arrived in the United States for training. Each gun had different-colored bullets, so after the training exercises, the instructors could tell which guns were hitting the target.

"Unfortunately, the B-24 didn't have an interpreter on board," she says. "The Chinese thought they were to shoot at the plane [instead of the towed target].

"We got back with bullets in us, but we flew all right," she tells me with her typical wry humor.

Thirty-eight WASPs died in training during the war. Despite their honorable service, the WASPs were not accorded military status until 1977.

Overseas, Russia's women were also lobbying for the opportunity to fly for the military. Many were initially rejected and had to repeat their requests again and again. Thanks to the tireless efforts of a few and the intrepid commitment of the aspiring aviatrixes, the Russians developed three unique all-female regiments, the most famous of which was called "The Night Witches," or the 588th Aviation Regiment (later called the 46th Taman Guards Night Bomber Regiment). All told, the female regiments flew over twenty-three thousand sorties, dropping over three thousand tons of bombs and twenty-six thousand incendiary shells. Twenty-three pilots were honored with the title Hero of the Soviet Union, and several earned the designation of Fighter Ace.

Both the WASPs and the Russian regiments had the audacity to insist that they were capable of contributing at a time and in a way that challenged society's norms. Their surety had to come from within.

Honoring the Voice Inside

Remaining true to the values you hold dear and knowing which opportunities to pursue—as well as which ones to let pass—requires you to listen to what several women I interviewed referred to as their inner voice. For some of the leaders I interviewed for this book, that inner voice is what ultimately determined their decision to retire or move on.

Dee McWilliams tells the story of hearing that voice for herself toward the end of her career.

"My four-star boss came back from a meeting at the Pentagon to determine new assignments for generals," she says. "He told me they wanted me to stay in Germany for another year, and then go back to the Pentagon for a third star. I told him I had a decision to make and would come back with an answer.

"I knew I'd be going back to Rumsfeld's Pentagon, which was gearing up for a war that I felt would be a quagmire," she continues. "Colleagues in intelligence confided that there was no connection to WMDs. My conscience couldn't handle the deceit operating at the highest levels. I determined that it would destroy my moral core to participate in the process. Additionally, I had always promised myself that when the small voice inside whispered that it was time to go that I would listen and comply. I did."

As with anything of value, it can be hard to continue to listen to, hear, and honor that inner voice, the one that's connected to your values and to your core purpose—but that inner voice is absolutely critical to operating with grit. Your anchor mentor can help you cut through the noise and make the decisions that are true to you. It's also important to ensure that you give yourself adequate time for reflection, for reconnecting to your story and core purpose, and ensuring that the story you're living is in concert with the person you know yourself to be.

Connecting Actions to Values

1. Depth psychology—an interdisciplinary field and a concept pioneered by Eugen Bleuler to describe psychoanalytic approaches to therapy taking the unconscious into account—supposes that the person we wanted to be when we were children is an important North Star for who we want to be as adults. Yet this version of ourselves can sometimes be subsumed by the ego as we mature. To reorient yourself to this early vision, sit down with a pen and paper, and think back to when you were a child. What did you want to do? Who did you want to be? What was important to you? What values were important to you then, and what is important to you now? How has it changed, and why? Is there something you have not realized that you would like to bring back into your life?

2. Consider an action or a decision you regret because it was not in concert with who you were. What were the factors influencing that decision? Can you see, in hindsight, precisely how it was misaligned with your values? How might you do it differently if you were faced with a similar situation again? It's nearly impossible to learn from negative experiences without looking to see what contributed to them and how we were off-base in our thinking. Give yourself the gift of clarity now. It will help you the next time you face a decision that affects your values.

3. Consider a decision or an action you have pending—something big, such as choosing to accept a new position, asking for a promotion, or letting someone go. Then sit down and write for ten minutes about what matters most to you—outside of that action or decision. Now consider your decision in light of what you have written.

— 8 —

Above All, Be Adaptable

"It's not your fault, but it is your fight."

—Brigadier General Rebecca Halstead

"Never give in, never give in, never, never, never give in."

—Winston Churchill

Marine helicopter door gunner Kirstie Ennis was midway through her second deployment to Afghanistan in June of 2012 when her aircraft was shot down. Everything she thought she knew changed.

Ennis had grown up the daughter of two Marines, and confesses that as a kid, "I was pretty much a hellion." As soon as Ennis graduated high school, at age seventeen, she asked her parents to sign the waiver allowing her to enlist. They weren't excited about her choice.

"You can sign it now, or wait eight months until I turn eighteen, but I'm doing this," she told them. They reluctantly agreed.

Ennis became a gunner on the CH-53D, a heavy-lift helicopter manufactured by Sikorsky. Her job was "the most bad-to-the-bone job in the Marine Corps you can possibly have," she says. She loved the Marines. She loved the mission.

If there is an image in your head of what a Marine looks like—even a female Marine—Ennis likely does not match it. She is petite and athletic, with long, wavy blond hair that falls midway down her back. Perhaps more in line with the typical image of a Marine is the large tat on her back that she shared with the world on the cover of *ESPN* magazine in 2017—at first glance a feminine design complete with flowers, birds, and a heart. But when you look more closely, you see two well-dressed skulls—one in a top hat, the other in a veil—and the words *Semper Fidelis*, the Marine Corps motto ("always faithful"), etched in her skin.

Those words enforce Ennis's sense of connection to the Marine mission and to her fellow Marines. As she puts it: "I protect my helicopter. And I protect the men and women who get on my helicopter."

For her second deployment, Ennis's unit was stationed at Camp Leatherneck, in the Helmand Province of Afghanistan, the largest of thirty-four provinces. Though its culture dates back to the third millennium BC, Helmand today is populated by a rural, agricultural tribal society with a literacy rate barely in the double digits. Almost no households have clean water. Helmand is one of the world's largest opium-producing regions. For Americans, it is the most dangerous region of Afghanistan.

From the very start, Ennis felt that her second deployment was different. The operational tempo was quicker than in her first deployment. "Every other day I was going out, and every time it was different." Also, "I was flying a lot more days [as opposed to nights]," she says.

Daytime flights are a loaded subject for those who fly on military helicopters. Helicopters are loud and slow, and benefit from the cover of darkness that night missions provide. Predictably, "there's also a lot more engagement during the day," Ennis says, referring to enemy contact.

On June 23, 2012, Ennis had a bad feeling about that day's mission—a combat resupply and an extraction of Marines. What should have been routine felt off.

Just hours before the mission, Ennis was pulled off her helicopter and reassigned to Irontail 06, a different helicopter, which was named in memoriam for a crew of six Marines who had been shot down and killed before the start of Ennis's second deployment.

At launch time, she climbed into the back and tethered herself to the aircraft with the gunner's belt, just as she always did. The blades cut into the desert air, and the helicopter lifted off into the dusk.

The crew was only partway into the mission when there was a sudden and violent flash of light. The nose of the aircraft pitched upward. Ennis felt the helicopter falling. There was nothing she could do. "I'm going to die," she thought.

She lost consciousness. When Ennis opened her eyes, all she could hear were screams. She tried to scream, but couldn't—too much blood clogged her nose and throat. A corpsman ran to her and yelled at her to stay awake, not to close her eyes. He could see what Ennis could only feel: her lower jaw had been ripped off. Her teeth were gone. Her arms were useless. Her left leg was mangled, her spine damaged. As if this weren't brutal enough, the corpsmen wouldn't give her painkillers, concerned about possible brain damage.

Ennis's first surgery was in Afghanistan, followed by dozens more in Germany, and then still more at Walter Reed Hospital in Bethesda, Maryland. Finally, she was brought back to Balboa Medical Center in San Diego. It was the first time she'd seen her parents. Her father was in tears, and "my father never cries," she says.

Despite it all, "I was determined to recover so I could go back and fight," she says.

Around this time, the doctors realized she had frontal-lobe damage as well.

"Nobody could explain what was going on inside my head," she says. "I couldn't recover words. Huge chunks of my memory had vanished. I had to do speech therapy. I was jumpy, anxious, besieged by flashbacks. The slightest noise, the rumble of a truck passing by, and I was back in the helicopter shattered on the ground, blood pouring from my mouth."[1]

Despite her commitment to recovery and her love of the Marines, it became clear that Ennis would never fight again. At the one-year anniversary of the crash, Ennis tried to take her own life. When her father came to see her in the hospital, he was no longer sad, but angry.

"The enemy couldn't kill you, so you're going to do it yourself?" he asked.

"I'd lost my purpose," Ennis says (highlighting just how imperative and lifesaving is the work of drilling down to core purpose that we covered in chapter 2).

Around this time, an invitation from Disabled Sports USA introduced her to snowboarding, and she never looked back. "Snowboarding saved my life," she says.

Ennis also joined Walking with the Wounded on a one-thousand-mile walk in the United Kingdom, seventy-two days at twelve to fifteen miles a day. Then her leg became infected, and doctors had to amputate above the knee, bringing her total number of surgeries up to forty-four.

Ennis continues to persevere and set new goals for herself, driven by a modified version of her original purpose of serving her country. "I can't serve in the military, but I can still serve the military community," she says. Ennis established the Kirstie Ennis Foundation, which redistributes the sponsorship earnings she collects from her adventures to deserving charities.

Now Ennis is working toward a new goal: climbing the Seven Summits (the highest peaks on each of the seven continents). "Heck, I've been to the lowest. Why not take myself to the highest?" she quips. Her first attempt to climb Mount Everest failed, but she is not deterred.

How does Ennis find the grit to keep going? "I don't look backward. It is a blessing and a curse," she confesses. She also offers these words of encouragement and admonition to others: "When it comes to the body, it's what's between the ears and beneath the ribcage that counts." Finally, "Nobody owes you anything. You owe it to yourself."

Navigating the Changes That Rock You to Your Core

This chapter is about big change—its challenges and its opportunities. It is about recovering from the unexpected. Discussing the work of living—and thriving—through change falls near the end of this book for a reason: it takes all of the work of the preceding chapters to be able to successfully navigate unexpected change. This change may be welcome or unwelcome—either will require careful maneuvering. Whether change comes in a moment or as a result of a decision, your success comes from the work you have done in defining your story, drilling down to your core purpose, and staying connected to your values. You may refine your mission, but you won't lose sight of it altogether. You may stay on course or make changes based on circumstance. Making that decision is part of the ability to adapt.

For some leaders, especially those who are accustomed to success or who have tied their identities to their jobs or to some other aspect of life that is altered, accepting that a door has been closed or a road diverted is almost too much to bear. Change is challenging in part because it illuminates the tension between the desire for and yet the illusion of control. Adaptability is finding the way to work within that tension.

The ability to persist in the face of extreme change and challenge is what Nick Tasler, organizational psychologist and author of *Ricochet: What to Do When Change Happens to You,* calls adaptive leadership. Considering a study of managers in the telecommunications industry in the wake of deregulation, Tasler notes that the thing that separated those who floundered from those who succeeded was adaptability.

"The adaptive leaders chose to view all changes, whether wanted or unwanted, as an expected part of the human experience, rather than as a tragic anomaly that victimizes unlucky people," Tasler writes. "Instead of feeling personally attacked by ignorant leaders, evil lawmakers, or an unfair universe, they remained engaged in their work and spotted opportunities to fix long-standing problems with customer service and to tweak antiquated pricing structures."[2]

Tasler's analysis reiterates just how critical your perspective on unexpected events can be. In the face of tragedy or setback, you can choose to be a victim (overwhelmed, incapacitated, unable to move forward) or a leader (finding ways to transform unfortunate circumstance into something of meaning). Successfully navigating this kind of change requires making use of the tempered optimism, mental agility, and self-regulation we covered in chapter 5. Adaptability may require you to reframe your story—and remain connected to purpose—choosing another path or even another direction, concepts we covered in chapters 1 and 2. If grit is a dogged determination in the face of difficult circumstance, adaptability means that this doggedness may require creativity in its execution. These tools can help anchor you even when you can't imagine how you will be able to persevere. They are the tools that steadied me when the ground fell out from under my feet.

The Power of Momentum

At the end of my eight-year commitment in uniform, I left the Army. A combination of many factors drove my decision. I had not found the camaraderie for which I had hoped. After several negative experiences, I had lost faith in the organization. Realizing that my flying days were largely behind me and that staff time is mostly what lay ahead, I was neither challenged nor fulfilled. I looked at those senior to me and did not find examples of where I wanted to go, or who I wanted to be. While deployed to Kuwait, on the last day that applications would be accepted, I submitted my application to the Tuck School at Dartmouth.

When I'd arrived at my final duty assignment, I notified my command of my intent to leave the Army at the end of my obligation. The Army was bleeding captains then, and the general officer in charge of my final unit of assignment asked me what he could offer to get me to stay. I replied, "A second command at Fort Carson in the Cavalry followed by a foreign area officer assignment." I thought it was a pipe dream. I didn't realize that when a general asks what he can do, it will be done. I received my orders the same day as my acceptance to Tuck.

It was a hard decision, and one I still feel a little bit guilty about. I went back to the factors that had driven my original intent to leave. I called my dad. "Just don't make this decision out of ego," he advised. A number of factors informed my decision in the end. My passion for the work had waned. I had not felt able to lead in a way congruent with the person I was. Moreover, I considered that this general would not be there each time the Army diverted my assignments, a common occurrence at a time when officers were leaving at such an accelerated rate. I accepted admission to business school. I drove away from Fort Bliss looking straight ahead down that Texas highway, and didn't look back.

I won't pretend that I didn't have doubts. A month after I left the Army, just after I began classes toward my MBA, on September 11, 2001, the Twin Towers fell. The world was plunged into chaos, the kind that I had trained for. I wanted to be a part of the solution. I remember a classmate, a Marine, and I watching the news about deployments while others talked about the hockey game that night and feeling a deep disconnect in purpose. I considered going back into the Army. But I'd made a thoughtful choice to leave. The Army was a big organization. It didn't need me. I had to live into my discomfort.

The grit-related question in this time of transition and uncertainty was how could I continue working connected to purpose without yet having a new mission? There was no answer in my immediate future. My work then was to take full advantage of the education I'd chosen and trust that continued introspection would help me find my path.

This isn't the change that toppled my world, though. I earned my MBA at Tuck, and went to work in the corporate world in the medical-device and technology industries. I expected life would settle into a comfortable rhythm. I lived in an apartment in a neighborhood in Seattle where I could go for runs and bikes along Lake Washington.

One weekend I visited my brother in Portland. That Sunday, the world as I knew it came to an end. Walking in the market with my brother, I had a phone call, followed by a text message ending with the numbers "9-1-1." I returned the call, and the police department in the remote village of Kaktovik, Alaska, answered.

I knew that my father and stepmother were kayaking in the Arctic National Wildlife Refuge in my home state of Alaska. I had talked to them on the satellite phone a week before, on Father's Day.

The voice on the other end of the line asked if I was Richard and Katherine's daughter.

I said that I was.

And then the voice said words I will never forget: "I'm sorry to tell you this," it said, "but a bear came into their campsite last night, and they were both killed."

Changes in my life until that point had been more gradual or mostly self-imposed. This time, change arrived in toto. Everything I thought I knew came crashing down around me.

In the short term, I needed immediate strategies for survival. Some days I didn't want to get out of bed or brush my teeth. I didn't want to pay bills or answer the phone. I cancelled trips I had planned, sometimes at the last minute. Some people understood, and others did not. It was important to take some time not only to do things that needed to be done but also to drastically reduce my obligations.

That Thanksgiving, I went to see my grandma on my father's side, and other relatives. I don't remember what triggered her comment, but at some point she and I sat in the kitchen talking together. I remember she looked at me with life-weary eyes, the same eyes my dad had, the same eyes that I have, and said slowly, "You just have to keep on keeping on."

Keep on keeping on? I thought. *That* was the best this wise woman could offer? I wanted a flash of soul-deep inspiration, a revelation about faith, something of substance!

I did not stop to think how deep her sorrow must have been then, losing her son. I was thinking only of my own loss. It took me a long time to understand how important her advice truly was. In the face of the inexplicable, the unbearable, the circumstances that would otherwise be paralyzing, sometimes the best you can do is put one foot in front of the other and remind yourself to breathe. You have to keep moving. You have to keep on keeping on.

This advice may sound basic, but it is still difficult to follow. For a period of time, your purpose may become simply forward movement. Your strength alone is not enough, and you may have to rely on momentum to get you through. When you scrape rock bottom, you push off just to keep going. Sometimes, putting one foot in front of the other is a triumph. With each step you take— no matter how tentative or small—you say, "I will not quit."

Finding Creative Ways Forward

There is a recurring theme in the stories of all the women I interviewed for this book, a recurrence hinting at the intensity of the challenges endured. If one remark appears in interview after interview, it is, "I just won't quit."

Most every woman I spoke with had at least one moment in which she had to decide that she was not giving up. This determination may have been tested many times, but in each case, the leaders interviewed in this book refused to even consider quitting as an option. This idea came out so pointedly in so many conversations that it became clear that in difficult times, moving forward was itself the goal.

I hope to have brought you to the same realization—that no matter the circumstance or situation, you have the tools, the insight, and the inspiration you need to continue onward, despite how many unexpected turns your path may take or how many obstacles you may encounter. Adaptability, the ability to work in changing environments, was critical to the grit shown by each leader we've considered. This may be in response to a discrete incident—consider Karen Fine Brasch failing the obstacle course or Dee McWilliams's commander vulgarly propositioning her—or it may result from a more sustained circumstance, such as Ann Dunwoody working in a job well beneath her qualifications or Sara Faulkner's career-long experience of hostile work environments.

Change is not always traumatic. It can come in unexpected yet positive ways, too, and the ability to prepare for and adapt to a positive turn is equally important. That's what Lieutenant Commander Krysten Ellis, whose story I shared in chapter 3, faced at the start of her military career.

You recall that Ellis was the daughter of a submariner. She wanted nothing more than to serve on a submarine, but when she joined the Navy, women weren't allowed to serve on submarines. Ellis became a supply officer for the Navy instead. While she was serving as a supply officer, the opportunity arose for women to teach at the Naval Nuclear Power School (NPS) in Goose Creek, South Carolina, where sailors learn to operate the nuclear weapons often carried by submarines. Yet still, women were restricted from serving on subs. Ellis applied for, and got, the assignment.

Then the opportunity she had most hoped for became reality. On April 29, 2010, the Department of the Navy announced a policy change that would allow women to begin serving on submarines. The combination of specializing in supply and teaching at NPS positioned Ellis perfectly to transition into a submarine billet.

Even after receiving the clearance to serve on a submarine, Ellis had to go through a year and a half of rigorous training—training Cleve Langdale, a former nuclear machinist's mate, characterized as "white walls, PowerPoint and fluorescent lighting . . . four to six years of college-level information [crammed] into a six-month period."[3]

The classroom portion of the training is mentally and physically grueling, as reported by Langdale: "People would stand up during class and post themselves at podiums in the rear, just so they could stay awake. Every now and then one of them would literally fall over. Many times I'd be watching a lecture and hear a boom as the person standing behind me collapsed and took his podium with him. On the plus side, the rest of us would be quite awake after that . . . for maybe five minutes."

Ellis endured the training, and moved on to the challenges of life on a submarine. Sailors switch to an eighteen-hour day: sleep six hours, work six hours, study six hours.

"Everyone's just trying to get their quals [qualifications], their dolphins [the insignia that connotes completion of submarine training]," Ellis says. "You might do a six-hour shift, then your regular job, and then tasks toward your qual. There were a few months where I didn't sleep more than two or three hours a night."

Ellis served two tours on submarines, all because she was adaptable enough to take every opportunity to work toward her goal, even when that goal appeared to be out of reach. She prepared and excelled so that when the change came that she had dreamed of, she was ready for it. Even though her path was by turns arduous and winding, and her ultimate goal appeared impossible at times, her refusal to give up—and her willingness to take a more creative path—led to success.

Using Grit for Good

This book is about leadership, and it is about grit. They are important and necessary elements of success, especially if you are in a particularly inhospitable work environment, or if you're going through times of change and transformation either in an industry or in your own career, or both.

By themselves, of course, leadership and grit do not have moral value. There are those people we've all read about, studied, or perhaps even known who have these characteristics and apply them toward ends that do not serve the world. A recent example comes in the 2019 documentary *The Great Hack*, an exposé of the data-harvesting firm Cambridge Analytica and its role in the 2016 presidential election and Brexit vote and the implications of the firm's work on the future of privacy. The film introduces a key Cambridge Analytica employee who applied her skills and her fortitude toward something that did (and continues to do) great harm in the world. The documentary reveals her change of heart and desire to set things right. It also makes clear that it will be impossible for her to repair all the damage that she helped to facilitate.

Celebrated American writer and theologian Frederick Buechner suggests that our goal should be to find that place where "your deep gladness and the world's deep hunger coincide."[4] To understand your own deep gladness, regularly revisit and stay connected to the values embedded in your story and your core purpose. Ask yourself, How can I use what I love to contribute to the greater good?

What drove the leaders interviewed in this book more than anything else was the belief that their service and sacrifice were making a tangible, positive difference. Some of them connected with the military mission, some with the more general concept of service, and all connected with taking care of people. For many, they understood that their example would be a light for other women to follow, and would reveal to men how powerful women's contributions could be. These points of connection did not mitigate the difficulties, but they made the difficulties worth the challenge. And when these women no longer felt that they were making a difference, or when they no longer were connected to the mission (or were in some cases directly opposed to it), they made a change. It was time to move on; to change the arena where they sought to have a positive impact.

This doesn't mean that every challenge you undertake must serve the greater good. It's worth it to work toward that promotion, to ask for that stretch assignment. Developing in your field in any way will allow you to have greater impact. It's instructive to take on goals outside of work, too—perhaps training for a road race or learning a new language. Developing your ability to confront and work through trials becomes a part of your story, and helps you build grit and confidence for any endeavor.

Discerning the answers to these questions is work for a lifetime, but it is never too soon (or too late) to begin it. Doing the work to stay in alignment with your answers is similarly permanent, even though your circumstances will change. Many of the leaders I interviewed who have completed their time in the service are finding ways to give back out of uniform. They have internalized the importance of service, and they learn that being in uniform is not the only way to inhabit that mandate.

When it is time to move on from an experience, new challenges will be no less difficult, only different. And that is where adaptability comes into play. It is what enables you to take the lessons you have learned from your earlier experiences and apply them to new situations.

The first day I walked out onto the flight line all those years ago in Alabama, I drew strength from knowing I had done hard things before. I remembered that final summit push on Denali, struggling to take each step at nineteen thousand and then twenty thousand feet. At these elevations, the air contains less than half the oxygen it does at sea level, and every step was a concerted act of will. I forced my breath out with each step, pushing the oxygen into my bloodstream. I sucked in as much air as I could. I set my crampon down into the ice and snow and rocked forward to shift my weight onto my skeletal structure so that my muscles would have some relief. Every step seemed impossible, and yet every step brought me that much closer to the summit.

My guide, John, and I stood for just a couple of minutes at the top of the continent. The icy peaks of the Alaska Range stretched as far as I could see in every direction. There was nothing more beautiful at that moment than acknowledging that I'd used all I had, every ounce to get to the summit. But most accidents happen on the descent, so any elation had to be short-lived. Sheer focus and will brought us, step by cramponed step, down the three thousand feet of ice to high camp. The next day we pushed the rest of the way down the mountain to base camp.

That experience on an icy mountain supported each step I took onto that flight line. I recalled the challenge and the triumph, and I knew I could get through what seemed impossible. When I climbed into the cockpit for the first time and sat for just a moment in equal amounts of excitement and sheer terror, I remembered how I had jumped from an airplane, flown at terminal velocity, deployed my parachute, and landed safely under canopy over a hundred times.

As I've grown older, challenges related to thrill are less interesting to me, and those related to purpose are increasingly important. I've felt a palpable change from external motivations to those coming from inside; a transmutation from interest in individual pursuit to something that connects directly to making positive contributions. When I accepted a job at Microsoft in my thirties, I felt embarrassed to tell anybody where I was working. There was nothing wrong with working there. It's a great company. I learned a lot, contributed a lot, and worked with many great people. But I knew that the work wasn't aligned with who I was and what was most important to me—I was out of touch with my core purpose and my authentic self. It was not work that represented the intersection of my desires and the world's needs. Something inside me was beginning to shift.

My father and stepmother were killed six months after I began working at Microsoft. For a while, I relied on momentum alone. I understood in a way I could not have before how short life could be. I started to feel a mandate to use the gifts I had to make a difference in whatever time I was allotted.

While at Microsoft, I began studies toward a master of divinity, and then decided to focus on writing. I worked on the book that would become *North of Hope*. I began a low-residency program toward a master of fine arts, and left Microsoft to focus on writing. As I look back on that time of change now, I think of it as a continually evolving discernment of purpose, a realization that—as Socrates reportedly said—the unexamined life is not worth living. My original work had required me to align to its goals and objectives. Now I had the opportunity to figure out what drove me, where I could best contribute.

Writing and other creative work has always been a source of deep gladness for me. I also didn't want to let go of the years of experience in business and, before that, operations. I put together a presentation for a women's business group and offered it free as a lunchtime education session. The rest, as they say, is history, though of course history means years of continuing to understand and refine the lessons that came from this time. I drew on mentors in my new focus area of speaking. I asked questions and listened. I put hours and hours into every task. In short, I used the tools and skills acquired from years in uniform, in the cockpit, and in the boardroom to test and develop this new direction.

In David Epstein's book *Range*, he talks about the enduring success of the generalist, and how adaptability to changing interest and direction often leads to success while building a solid foundation, all the stronger for its being constructed of learning from many pursuits.[5] Many of the most successful people he studied are focused more on the short term than the long term, allowing themselves to pivot to new interests and directions. Each new position informs the next. Although the road may be windy, the breadth of experience gained along the way supports stronger performance in later work. The key attribute to this kind of success is adaptability.

I don't know that I would have originally looked over my story and seen how well mentorship and teaching fit into the arc of my experience, but in this process of refinement I came to realize that my journey now is less about blazing trails and more about finding ways to help others. My speaking and my writing allow me to exercise creativity (a core value unrealized in earlier work) and earn a living while making a difference in a way I never would have anticipated before, in a way that only came about because of hard work, good fortune, a supportive family, and remaining open to opportunity.

This adaptability and discernment is not only for the professional realm. Six years ago, my family and I moved to a smaller community from the big city because we wanted, as a family, to live more within our values, one of which was to spend time in wild places, and another of which was to spend time with each other. Both my husband and I are entrepreneurs, so our days have an urgency that wasn't present in the corporate setting— nobody else cares whether or not we get our work done. We drive ourselves. This suits us both. With less time spent traversing the busy city streets, we also have more time with our two active boys. For several years I've donated my free time (and some of my sanity) toward funding and building a new library in our small community. We founded and run an Episcopal lay-led fellowship. None of these ventures are without their challenges and requirements. All require grit in one way or another—sometimes a lot. Each pursuit informs our other work.

Life is no less busy, but it is more fulfilling. The winding road of this journey has led me to a place where I still struggle to balance the various demands, but grit comes more naturally because I've built my life around what I love and where I know I can contribute.

This is what I hope for you—that in developing these skills and training your mindset, you embark on a journey to find the place where the world needs you the most, where you are focused on applying your ever-evolving toolkit in accordance with your core purpose, aligned with your values, and in service of leaving this planet a little better for your having walked here. When you encounter challenges—as each of us will, repeatedly—remember that when you face into the wind, the resistance will help you to rise.

Notes

Chapter 1

1. Maria Tatar, "The Great Cauldron of Story: Why Fairy Tales Are for Adults Again," interview by Krista Tippett, *On Being with Krista Tippett* (March 13, 2013).

2. Marshall Ganz, "Leading Change: Leadership, Organization, and Social Movements," in *Handbook of Leadership Theory and Practice*, eds. Nitin Nohria and Rakesh Khurana (Boston: Harvard Business School Publishing, 2010), 527.

3. David Comer Kidd and Emanuele Castano, "Reading Literary Fiction Improves Theory of Mind," *Science* 342, no. 6156 (2013): 377.

4. Dan P. McAdams, "The Role of Narrative in Personality Psychology Today," *Narrative Inquiry* 16, no. 1 (2006): 11.

5. Michael S. Gazzaniga, "The Interpreter Within: The Glue of Conscious Experience," *Cereberum*, April 1, 1999.

6. Sinéad L. Mullally and Eleanor A. Maguire, "Memory, Imagination, and Predicting the Future," *The Neuroscientist* 20, no. 3 (2014): 220.

7. Claudia J. Kennedy, *Generally Speaking* (New York: Warner Books, 2001).

8. Ibid., 68.

9. Julie Beck, "Life's Stories," *The Atlantic*, August 10, 2015.

Chapter 2

1. John Spencer, "The Challenges of Ranger School and How to Overcome Them," Modern War Institute at West Point, April 12, 2016, https://mwi.usma.edu/challenge-ranger-school-can/; Special Operations Forces Report (SOFREP), "How It Really Went Down in the First Class to Graduate Female Rangers," August 21, 2015, https://mwi.usma.edu/challenge-ranger-school-can/.

2. Angela Duckworth, *Grit* (New York: Scribner, 2016), 148.

3. Aaron Hurst, "CEOs—'2020 Tipping Point for Purpose Economy,'" *Psychology Today*, January 25, 2016.

4. Darlene M. Iskra, *Breaking through the Brass Ceiling* (La Vergne, TN: Lightning Source, 2008), 118.

5. "Leadership Quotes," https://govleaders.org/quotes.htm, accessed March 31, 2020.

6. Tom Peters, "You Must Care," TPG Communications, 1987, https://tompeters.com/columns/you-must-care.

7. Rebecca Halstead, *24-7: The First Person You Must Lead Is Yourself* (Scott's Valley, CA: CreateSpace Independent Publishing Platform, 2013).

8. Jeff Rhodes, "KC-130J Harvest Hawk Operations in Afghanistan," *Code One*, December 12, 2012, http://www.codeonemagazine.com/article .html?item_id=112.

Chapter 3

1. Chris Weller, "A Neuroscientist Who Studies Decision-Making Reveals the Most Important Choice You Can Make," *Business Insider,* July 28, 2017.

2. Anthony Tjan, *Good People: The Only Leadership Decision That Really Matters* (New York: Portfolio, 2017), 217–220.

3. Darlene Marie Iskra, "Breaking through the 'Brass' Ceiling: Elite Military Women's Strategies for Success" (PhD diss., University of Maryland, 2007), 40–41.

4. Thomas J. DeLong, John J. Gabarro, and Robert J. Lees, "Why Mentoring Matters in a Hypercompetitive World," *Harvard Business Review,* January 2008.

5. Sameer B. Srivastava, "Network Intervention: Assessing the Effects of Formal Mentoring on Workplace Networks," *Social Forces* 94, no. 1 (2015): 427.

6. Tammy D. Allen et al., "Career Benefits Associated with Mentoring for Protégés: A Meta-Analysis," *Journal of Applied Psychology* 89, no. 1 (2004): 127.

7. John Stuart Mill, *The Principles of Political Economy: With Some of Their Applications to Social Philosophy*, bk. v, ch. xvii, sec. 3 (1848) in: *The Collected Works of John Stuart Mill*, vol. 3, p. 594.

8. Alice Eagly and Linda Carli, *Through the Labyrinth: The Truth about How Women Become Leaders* (Boston: Harvard Business Review Press, 2007).

9. Julia Fawal, "The Five Types of Mentors You Need in Your Life," TED-Ed blog, October 9, 2018, https://blog.ed.ted.com/2018/10/09/the -5-types-of-mentors-you-need-in-your-life/.

10. Lauren Bidwell, "Why Mentors Matter: A Summary of 30 Years of Research," SAP SuccessFactors, accessed September 9, 2019, https://www

.successfactors.com/content/ssf-site/en/resources/knowledgc-hub/why-mentors-matter.html.

11. SEC archives (2017): 2016 Letter to Amazon Shareholders from CEO Bezos.

Chapter 4

1. Kestutis Kveraga, Avniel S. Ghuman, and Moshe Bar, "Top-Down Predictions in the Cognitive Brain," *Brain and Cognition* 65, no. 2 (2007): 145.

2. David Bicllo, "Back to the Future: How the Brain 'Sees' the Future," *Scientific American*, January 2, 2007.

3. Jerome Groopman, *How Doctors Think* (New York: Mariner Books, 2007).

4. *Master Resilience Training Participant Guide* (Philadelphia: University of Pennsylvania, 2014), 120.

5. Tom Peters, *The Excellence Dividend* (New York: Vintage Books, 2018).

6. Brené Brown, *Dare to Lead* (New York: Random House, 2018), 49.

7. Anthony K. Tjan, "Learning Optimism with the 24x3 Rule," hbr.org, July 26, 2011, https://hbr.org/2011/07/learning-optimism-with-the-24x.html.

8. Rosabeth Moss Kanter, "Management by Flying Around," hbr.org, September 21, 2009, https://hbr.org/2009/09/mbfa-management-by-flying-arou.html.

9. Anita L. Tucker and Sara J. Singer, "The Effectiveness of Management-by-Walking-Around: A Randomized Field Study," working paper 12-113, Harvard Business School, Boston, 2013.

Chapter 5

1. Alexandra Hemmerly-Brown, "Female POWs Prove Women Can Endure War's Hardships," US Army News Service, March 31, 2011.

2. Rhonda Cornum and Peter Copeland, *She Went to War: The Rhonda Cornum Story* (Novato, CA: Presidio Press, 1993).

3. Rick Musselman, "Comprehensive Soldier Fitness Program Builds Strength, Resiliency," *Belvior* (Virginia) *Eagle*, March 1, 2012, https://www.army.mil/article/74853/comprehensive_soldier_fitness_program_builds_strength_resiliency.

4. Donald S. Hiroto and Martin E. Seligman, "Generality of Learned Helplessness in Man," *Journal of Personality and Social Psychology* 31, no. 2 (1975): 311.

Notes

Notes

5. "Resilience Skill Set," University of Pennsylvania, School of Arts and Sciences, Positive Psychology Center, https://ppc.sas.upenn.edu/resilience-programs/resilience-skill-set, accessed April 1, 2020.

6. Jim Collins, *Good to Great* (New York: HarperCollins, 2001), 83–85.

7. Laura Aiuppa Denning, Marc Meisnere, and Kenneth E. Warner, eds., *Preventing Psychological Disorders in Service Members and Their Families: An Assessment of Programs* (Washington, DC: National Academies Press, 2014).

8. "Master Resilience Training Skills," U.S. Army Reserve, https://www.usar.army.mil/MRT, accessed February 12, 2019.

9. Erin McShane, *Shave Your Head: A Female Ranger Graduate Answers Your Questions* (self-published, 2019).

10. *Master Resilience Training Participant Guide* (Philadelphia: University of Pennsylvania, 2014).

11. Atul Gawande, *The Checklist Manifesto* (New York: Metropolitan Books, 2009), 13.

12. Francesca Gino and Michael I. Norton, "Why Rituals Work," *Scientific American*, May 14, 2013.

Chapter 6

1. "Director's Advisory Group on Women in Leadership Unclassified Report," Central Intelligence Agency, March 2013.

2. Marianne S. Waldrop, "Understanding Women Leaders in a Male-Dominated Profession: A Study of the United States Marine Corps' Women Generals" (PhD diss., University of San Diego, 2016).

3. "Coast Guard Heroes: Alda Siebrands," video, 6:23, http://www.coastguardchannel.com/original-series/coast-guard-heroes/alda-siebrands/.

4. Anne Kreamer, "Not Taking Risks Is the Riskiest Career Move of All," hbr.org, April 16, 2015, https://hbr.org/2015/04/not-taking-risks-is-the-riskiest-career-move-of-all.

5. Catherine H. Tinsley and Robin J. Ely, "What Most People Get Wrong about Men and Women," *Harvard Business Review*, May–June 2018.

6. Victoria L. Brescoll, Erica Dawson, and Eric Luis Uhlmann, "Hard Won and Easily Lost: The Fragile Status of Leaders in Gender-Stereotype-Incongruent Occupations," *Psychological Science* 21, no. 11 (2010): 1640.

7. Carol S. Dweck, *Mindset: The New Psychology of Success* (New York: Ballantine Books, 2006).

8. "Dr. Dweck's Research into Growth Mindset Changed Education Forever," Mindset Works, https://www.mindsetworks.com/science, accessed April 2, 2020.

210

Chapter 7

1. Katty Kay and Claire Shipman, "The Confidence Gap," *The Atlantic*, May 2014.

2. Pauline Rose Clance and Suzanne Ament Imes, "The Imposter Phenomenon in High Achieving Women: Dynamics and Therapeutic Intervention," *Psychotherapy: Theory, Research & Practice* 15, no. 3 (1978): 241.

3. Carol A. Gallagher and Susan K. Golant, *Going to the Top: A Road Map for Success from America's Leading Women Executives* (New York: Viking, 1999).

4. Deborah L. Rhode, "Facing the Double Bind," *Perspectives* 10 (2002): 2.

5. Alice H. Eagly and Linda L. Carli, *Through the Labyrinth* (Boston: Harvard Business School Publishing, 2007).

6. Juliana Menasce Horowitz, Ruth Igielnik, and Kim Parker, "Women and Leadership 2018: Section 2: Views on Leadership Traits and Competencies and How They Intersect with Gender," Pew Research Center, September 20, 2018.

7. Carol Barkalow, *In the Men's House* (New York: Poseidon Press, 1990).

8. Ibid.

9. Richard M. Ryan and Edward L. Deci, "On Happiness and Human Potentials: A Review of Research on Hedonic and Eudaimonic Well-Being," *Annual Review of Psychology* 52, no. 1 (2001): 141.

10. Francesca Gino, *Rebel Talent* (New York: Dey Street Books, 2018).

11. Jim Harter, "Employee Engagement on the Rise in the U.S.," Gallup, August 26, 2018, https://news.gallup.com/poll/241649/employee-engagement-rise.aspx.

12. Francesca Gino, "How to Make Employees Feel Like They Own Their Work," hbr.org, December 7, 2015, https://hbr.org/2015/12/how-to-make-employees-feel-like-they-own-their-work.

13. Linn Van Dyne and Jon L. Pierce, "Psychological Ownership and Feelings of Possession: Three Field Studies Predicting Employee Attitudes and Organizational Citizenship Behavior," *Journal of Organizational Behavior* 25, no. 4 (2004): 439.

Chapter 8

1. Kirstie Ennis, "A Wounded Marine Finds New Mountains to Climb," *Guideposts*, June 25, 2018.

2. Nick Tasler, "How to Get Better at Dealing with Change," hbr.org, September 21, 2016, https://hbr.org/2016/09/how-to-get-better-at-dealing-with-change.

3. Robert Evans and Cleve Langdale, "6 Things Movies Don't Show You about Life on a Submarine," *Cracked*, January 31, 2014, https://www.cracked .com/personal-experiences-1276-6-things-movies-dont-show-you-about-life -submarine.html#.

4. Frederick Buechner, *Wishful Thinking: A Theological ABC* (New York: Harper & Row, 1973).

5. David Epstein, *Range: Why Generalists Triumph in a Specialized World* (New York: Riverhead Books, 2019).

Index

Index

Acknowledgments

Writing this book came about after several years of interviewing women in the vanguard of their military fields and sharing their stories through a blog. Taking that material, synthesizing the lessons and doing the necessary research to develop and support them, and then crafting the results into a book was a huge feat—one that could not have happened without the assistance of a varied team of talented people.

Most of all, I am deeply grateful to each of the leaders who are a part of *The Grit Factor* and its journey, willing to share their lessons and stories. Not only is it difficult for women leaders, often constrained by societal norms, to share their stories, but the military also effectively trains a mindset that subverts the individual story below the greater organization, making it difficult to offer one's experience for the benefit of others. Sharing stories, though, is a powerful and necessary support for leaders at all phases of their own journeys, and I'm so grateful for those leaders who were willing to offer their experience with candor and vulnerability. Given the constraints of form and page count, I was not able to include every leader's story in the final product, but each has played a critical role in my putting this book together in a manner best crafted for others to use. Thank you for opening your minds and hearts and for sharing so much of your lives.

There has also been other outstanding work done in this area, and I am particularly indebted to Darlene Iskra's excellent dissertation titled "Breaking through the 'Brass' Ceiling: Elite Military Women's Strategies for Success" (published in 2008), as well as Marianne Waldrop's dissertation titled "Understanding Women

Leaders in a Male-Dominated Profession: A Study of the United States Marine Corps' Women Generals." Both are cited in this book.

No book gets off the ground without others believing in the work, its greater potential, and the author. I am deeply grateful for the many people who have been a part of bringing this work to a much larger audience. Thank you to my fellow veteran and Tuck School strategy professor Chris Trimble for connecting me to Jacque Murphy, who was willing to take on this project and was invaluable in its initial formation and development. Thank you to Kate Hanley for helping find the right structure for these stories.

Finding the right publishing partner for a book is absolutely critical, and I could not be more thrilled with where *The Grit Factor* landed. Thank you especially to Jeff Kehoe and the remarkable team at Harvard Business Review Press for so expertly stewarding *The Grit Factor* to the place where you are reading it today. Jeff's vision ensured each subsequent version of the book would speak to readers. Stephani Finks and the design team did an incredible job with the jacket, and Brandon Hill's photography is unmatched. Anne Starr and Jon Zobenica's thoughtful attention to detail and design helped to tighten and shape the final product.

Thank you also to Marsh Carter of MIT and Christine Sandler who agreed to be interviewed and share their decades of experience and learning to develop the chapter on mentorship.

Thank you to Nan Money, who offered comments and suggestions on the first version of the manuscript. And love and thanks to the studio of my writing friends—Tara Conklin, Allison Augustyn, and Margot Kahn Case—who are an ongoing source of support, both checking in and encouraging my work.

And always, my forever gratitude and love to my husband, Peter, and our two boys, Sam and Jude, who supported the days, weekends, evenings, and occasional insanity necessary to bring this project to fruition.

About the Author

SHANNON HUFFMAN POLSON is the founder and CEO of the Grit Institute, a leadership development organization focused on helping leaders thrive in times of change and uncertainty.

Polson was one of the first female attack pilots in the US Army. She led two Apache helicopter platoons and an aviation company on three different continents. She earned her MBA at the Tuck School of Business at Dartmouth and has worked at Microsoft and Guidant (now merged with Boston Scientific). She holds a BA from Duke University and an MFA in Creative Writing from Seattle Pacific University.

Polson is the author of *North of Hope: A Daughter's Arctic Journey*. She was recognized as a Trailblazer Woman of Valor by US Senator Maria Cantwell. She is an active community member and lover of libraries. She lives with her husband and their two boys in Washington State.